Training for Leadership

Training for Leadership

Brig. Parmodh Sarin
AOC (Retd.)

Manas Publications
New Delhi-110002 (INDIA)

MANAS PUBLICATIONS
(We Convert Fighters into Writers)
(Publishers-Library Suppliers-Importers & Exporters)
4402/5-A, Ansari Road (Opp. HDFC Bank)
Darya Ganj, New Delhi - 110 002 (India)
Phones: Off.: 011-23260783, 23265523, Res.: 011-23842660
E-mail: manaspublications@gmail.com
manaspub6@gmail.com
Website: www.manaspublications.in

New Impression 2016

ISBN : 978-81-7049-171-2

Rs. 495/-

Designed at: Manas Publications

Printed in India at
RK Print Services, Delhi
and published by Mrs Suman Lata for
Manas Publications, 4402/5-A,
Ansari Road, (Opp HDFC Bank),
Darya Ganj, New Delhi - 110 002 (INDIA)

Preface

"It is characteristic of the military mentality that non-human factors ... are held essential, while the human being, his desires and thoughts—in short, the psychological factors —are considered as unimportant and secondary". —Albert Einstein *Out of My Later Life*

My motives in taking up the subject of "Leadership" in the present times are largely defined when I highlight the issues involved in the 'Introduction'. Here it would be adequate to say that over the years, and more so after Independence in 1947, no other profession has had to move in all kinds of directions in concert with the changing times, as soldiering. The nature and history of all other professions as professions has been thoroughly dissected and elaborated upon by experts of different hues. Surprisingly, the professional character of the modern day military officer has been generally neglected. Independence, greater awareness and changing times have created a situation where there seems to be a mismatch between what is perceived to be the right approach to "Leadership" and what the environment demands. Is there something missing in our training, grooming and identification of those values that made the Indian Army what it has been? This question is my inspiration for this book on "Leadership".

Traditionally, an average Indian citizen has held a military officer in very high esteem. Collectively, the officer class has also lived up to the best traditions of its profession and the expectations of Indian people. Sustenance of this faith is what provides a sense of security to the common man. It gives him a feeling that his safety and the security of the nation are in safe hands. That is why on induction, an individual before he becomes an officer, is constantly reminded of the fact that this faith has to be sustained at all times. The military itself needs a constant reaffirmation of this public faith in their trustworthiness where the security and safety of the nation is concerned. A strengthening of this bond between the nation and the military can only be possible if the officers continue to hold these values as their 'talisman' under all conditions. We, as a country, seem to have lost track of the fact that high character in a military officer is what defines our national character. We seem to have ignored the fact that the military of a country-in its professional attitudes, its equipment, and its officers' corps -is an extension and a reflection of that country's society.

Public acceptance and admiration should have been enough for the youth of this country to automatically look for a career in the armed forces with all its attendant glory. But this is not happening. Any number of studies conducted by various agencies have established that the military is no longer the 'first career choice' of our youngmen, it is not even among the top ten in most cases. Apparently, something has somewhere gone wrong, and the faith that the people had in the uniform and the inspiration it provided to the youth seems to be flagging. Media exposures of corruption amongst those who handle procurements have only added to the already lowered esteem of the 'uniform'. This silent deterioration of the organisational clime can easily be discerned by a diligent and professional analysis. The problem (seemingly) is that the austerity of the military life is in conflict with the material comforts that the present generation looks for. This will be too simplistic a diagnosis of the issues involved. All democratic countries have faced this dilemma, because the values the military demands and the values our present day society holds dear are at odds with one another. Frankly, our society does not encourage those military virtues upon which in these trying times, and with an envious neighbourhood, the country has to depend. In terms of values, the youth of today value self-determination and control of their own work life more than the young people of earlier days did. Resultantly, personal values in concert and in conflict with the organisational values are posing a strong challenge to the traditional leadership requirements. In these changing times there does not appear to be a single pattern of behaviour that can be practised so as to yield consistently the best organisational performance under all conditions. My effort here is to suggest to the junior leader a methodology for responding to the environmental demands where conflict between what he is required to do and what he is expected to do, to succeed as a professional, is becoming more and more manifest.

In the military, special emphasis is being placed on the management of weapon systems, but there seems to be much less specific emphasis on the management of social systems. It is only in the case of machines where periodic maintenance, repairs and spares for efficient performance are enough to elicit a desired response. If you ignore them, or if you put them through excessive usage after you have done the maintenance bit they will continue to perform and respond so long as the maintenance cycle allows them to function. Feelings, emotions, love and affection are irrelevant where your guns and mortars are concerned. Humans require much more than "oil and lubrication" to make them respond, to put their heart and soul in the mission of soldiering. Traditional hierarchical relationships are under extreme pressure because the styles of yore and those methods of managing men are no longer sufficiently potent or acceptable to contemporary soldiering and soldiers. During my time, exhortations of Babar when his troops felt like running away from the battle or Alexander the Great's speeches to his soldiers were cited as examples of leadership. Today, more and more leaders tend to have greater reliance on graphs, charts and computer printouts. They fail to realise that if we could reduce everything to quantifiable factors, then achieving perfection and an ideal response from the 'led' should not be requiring any great effort. These commanders, seemingly, overlook the fact that in today's fast moving and ever changing world neither people, nor problems fit pre-defined moulds. To try and make the two fit distorts perceptions. The prescribed code of conduct is somewhat outdated. The institution of military service is in the need of laying down clear and contemporary policies on various aspects of military life. We need to develop a modern approach to soldierly conduct, which emphasises rational self-interest instead of relying upon the dogmatic and clearly obsolete invocations of devoutness and self-sacrifice. A sudden injection of concerned top leadership cannot repair the long drawn downslide nor can it create instant values cherished down the ages. Things have to start happening at the lower levels of leadership, that is where a subordinate actually interacts and forms an opinion about the quality and capability of those whose command he has to obey. To develop and nurture the art of controlling and expecting unflinching response from others in all kinds of situations requires a continuous and critical study of our military profession.

The social organisation (of the military in particular) today represents increased rationalisation, greater level of impersonality, less emphasis on traditional leadership and a lot on modern man-management techniques. I claim no expertise in 'human psychology' or any such sciences that direct and guide a leader's style and behaviour. Today, the theorists agree that no single trait or combination of traits make for a good leader. Instead, leaders are created by a combination of certain characteristics, as well as the external environment in which they find themselves. My effort is to bring those aspects which help one grow into a leader with an appropriate blend of pragmatism, realism and awareness. Awareness begins with three basic components: knowing your strength, knowing your weakness, and identifying those areas that need to be corrected before one is ready to be accepted as a leader of men. In this book I have tried to put those issues into focus that need immediate attention of leaders at different levels of the organisational structure.

It is no accident that the classical principles of organisation and administration that figure in management literature and are taught the world over seem to have emanated from the manuals of military administration in different parts of the world. It only seems that we, the military officers, have somehow either forgotten some of them, or are ignoring them in our hurry to get ahead in life. It will be appropriate that we recapitulate those principles and definitions that now guide the management world but basically are the tenets on which the military is designed and expected to function. In this book I have tried to blend various aspects of management that deal with people. The focus here is not only on the military and its man management. The topics discussed herein are applicable to any big sized industrial enterprise. The reader will find a large number of quotes from the 'industry leaders' who differentiated between "Leadership" and "Management" in their pursuit of excellence. Here it will suffice to say that management is essentially a matter of harmonising aims, circumstances and resources, so is leadership; that is if we propose to seriously differentiate between the two.

Qualities that basically are necessary in a leader of men, so as to enable him to motivate those under him, have been listed and examined at length by various authorities. I have taken a radical, rather than a traditional approach, to the issues involved. Therefore, I would not be surprised if some of the readers find me dogmatic, reactionary or even out of tune because what I am going to convey is not necessarily what they thought leadership is all about. This will be so because I feel that mixing modern thoughts on man management with a return to some of our time-tested and battle-honed precepts is necessary while dealing with today's soldiers, and more importantly, are essential for professional growth. The views I have pro-pounded are not just theoretical in nature. Management experts and generals who became legends in their lifetime have said (and practised in some form or the other) similar things. My premise is that old principles never die. They only need reviewing and renewing and where necessary redefining. Mine is an effort to make them contemporary, so to say. I have largely tried to update the old theories in the context of our present day society and the challenges and limitations that it imposes on the leader.

No matter how comprehensive the contents, it is doubtful that any single book can provide complete information and inputs on a subject as complex as 'leadership'. A serious practitioner of leadership has to keep his eyes and ears open all the time so as to imbibe what is necessary for his professional growth. This includes learning from our own experience and that of others who left their mark in different walks of society. This approach helps us in arriving at an understanding of how to apply basic principles governing leadership to specific situations. I have tried to give a generally normative view of the military profession keeping the ground realities in perspective. Throughout this book I have tried to describe leadership (some call it management) in terms of behavioural skills. What you do with whom and how, you know when and how to do it, is the crux. I have tried to be 'simple' and not 'simplistic' in what I am saying. A word of caution will also not be out of place. The reader who expects to be presented with an erudite, jargon filled exposition on leadership is in for a bit of disappointment. Because, being a run of the mill type, I, like most of my potential readers, hate the textbook approach and oversimplified solutions to the complex problem of providing leadership in today's environment. In this we will deal with the grooming and training of our leaders.

This effort of mine, I must emphasise, is not an indictment of the system of training and grooming of our leaders. Nor is it an apology for whatever is found to be wanting due to the times that we live in. Mine is an effort in practical terms to analyse the situation and put across ideas that could help a leader measure up to the organisational goals. Most of what I am going to say can be and will be challenged. But to totally disagree will also be challenging for an erudite reader who is also a leader, be it in the military or industry.

Brig Parmodh Sarin (Retd.)

Foreword

Every generation has had some excellent leaders (both in Military and Industry) and scholars who have practised leadership and have written on the subject. But there continues to be little consensus about what factors cause an individual's performance to inspire those placed under him. Academic theorists have produced a large number of leadership "models". These models appearing in various textbooks are backed by a lot of research and acumen. But the models cannot predict an individual's performance on the ground. If the leader is found wanting no amount of sophistication, training, or technology can help. The author here stipulates that what actually works is what one intuitively feels is correct or has experienced while growing in a leadership position.

Managers become leaders when they can master the behavioural skills necessary to fulfil the demanding requirements of different management positions. Only those managers who know how to shape behaviour effectively to fit ever changing organisational demands can flourish and become effective leaders. For this they have to be capable of rapid adaptation to changing circumstances. Understanding and accepting the imperfection of the system is what will help a leader to deliver. Brig P Sarin (Retd.) has dealt with all aspects of leadership in a manner that will encourage a thought process in that direction. This book, informative and instructive for leaders at various levels, should trigger discussions among practitioners of the art of leadership in spheres other than military as well.

The author's earlier work, *Military Logistics- The Third Dimension* gives a comprehensive account of all that it takes to make a military accept any professional challenge. It is only appropriate that he has now come up with this treatise on "Leadership". Leaders in all walks of life are going through difficult times. Military, in particular, has to find ways and means to ensure that the leaders remain totally focussed to their task in hand when there is a paradigm shift in the traditional value structure due to sudden and fast influx of materialism in different spheres. These practical insights into various facets that go in to making of a leader should be a big help to those who are in the business of providing leadership to people.

Maj. Gen. D.N. Khurana (Retd.)

Director General, All India Management Association

Acknowledgements

After my book Military Logistics-The Third Dimension" had seen the light of the day, some well-meaning friends suggested that I should take up "Leadership" as the next subject to write on. Their argument was that the modern technological revolution has confronted us with military problems of unprecedented complexity, problems made all the more difficult because of the social and political turbulence of the age in which we live. In these trying times it is somewhat difficult for a young leader (be it in the military or industry) to find for himself, what is successful leadership and why are some leaders more successful than others? I will be eternally grateful to these friends for sharing their practical experiences. Because of their generous efforts, this book is truer to both its subject and its potential reader. If I list them individually I might miss out on some; therefore I prefer to be generic.

I am grateful to Major General Nirmal Sondhi AVSM** (Retd.) and Air Vice Marshal K.C. Kapoor VSM (Retd.) for having examined the manuscript and for their practical suggestions for enhancing the readability and utility of this book. My special thanks are due to Maj. Gen. D.N. Khurana AVSM, (Retd.), Director General, All India Management Association (AIMA), who inspite of an exceptionally busy schedule, agreed to go through the manuscript. He is in the field of grooming leaders for the civil industry. His insights into the impact of what I have tried to convey on the subject are a big help in expanding the readership base.

In this endeavour I have also drawn heavily on experiences and writings of leaders from various armies of the world and those of the Industry who have influenced the growth and development of managers/leaders in a diverse range of fields. In fact, a glance at the bibliography, the list of articles and books to which I owe the inspiration for this book will inspire anyone interested in the subject of 'Leadership' in today's world seriously to go through the whole narrative.

Unless, specifically identified as the source, all the opinions expressed here are mine.

Some Important Definitions

Accountability is defined as the hard cold understanding that a man does his job or gets out of it.

Administration is the comprehensive effort to direct, guide and integrate associated human strivings, which are focussed towards some specific ends and aims.

Assertiveness refers to being forthright in expressing demands, opinions, feelings and attitudes.

Attachment means being dependent, either on someone or something. It is the result of identifying yourself too strongly with the external environment and other people, who could be your superiors, peers or subordinates. Attachment colours one's judgement and therefore may restrict a professional approach to people and situations.

Attitudes are learned pre-dispositions to respond to different situations in a predictable manner. Attitudes are normally governed by values.

Charisma is viewed as the process through which leaders arouse strong emotions in followers, an important outcome being the identification of the followers with the leader.

Control is "the ensuring that all which occurs is in accordance with the established rules and the instructions issued."

Culture is defined as the distinctive way of life of a group of people; it is their complete design of social and community existence. It is collective programming of the mind that distinguishes one group or category of people from another. A learned way of living, transmitted from one person to another down the years, not unchanged, yet with a particular fundamental underlying pattern, which is identifiable. It is the distinctive way of life of a group of people, their complete design for life.

Discipline is control from without. High morale leads to control from within, and creates an environment for self-discipline.

Ethics are standards of behaviour in relation to values as prescribed by tradition.

Espirit de corps is the sum total of discipline, training, instilling of and education of members of a unit. Comradeship and Regimental Spirit make up espirit de corps.

Ideology is an organisation of compatible beliefs, and it must be morally acceptable. Where 'belief' is concerned it must be rooted in the tradition of the country. Beliefs should be such that they are retained throughout life, even after soldiers have retired to normal civilian life.

Influence is the ability to affect behaviour of others in a particular direction.

Integrity is that quality of a man which requires that the only real purpose of any thought, word or deed is to build persons or things, in order to accomplish positive and ethical results.

Maturity is the balance between courage and consideration.

Mentor is someone who helps to develop the individual's potential, capability, judgement and wisdom. Senior officers must act as mentors to their youthful counterparts, trusting them with real responsibilities and allowing them to make their own decisions.

An organisation is the relation amongst its participants. These relations, like a man's muscles work best under tension.

Perception is interpretation-based data/knowledge. It is the chief mechanism by which human beings come to know the world outside themselves. It is an important facet of human behaviour as it helps one in interpretation of inputs obtained through various senses.

Planning is improvisation on a general sense of direction. "Long term planning" is not a panacea for lack of direction and vision.

Policy is a predetermined, selected course established as a guide towards accepted goals and objectives. Policies are set forth to allow many diverse individuals to make uniform and consistent decisions even when they are acting in virtually complete independence of one another.

Power is the strength to control or coerce someone to do something. Authority is power that is accepted as legitimate by subordinates.

Programmes represent simple or complex activities developed to carry out policies.

A procedure is defined as a series of related tasks that make up the chronological sequence and the established way of performing the work to be accomplished.

Quality Circle (QC). is a sub group formed by people from a work group whose job is to develop ways to better accomplish their task. It often means trying out new ideas.

Responsibility is the obligation of a person to carry out the assignments and functions given to him by a person of higher authority.

Rites and Rituals. Rites are relatively elaborate, dramatic and planned set of activities that combine various forms of cultural impressions that often have both practical and expressive consequences. Rituals are generally standardised procedures and have set techniques. These are performed in case of specific events and on particular occasions to keep the morale of the troops high.

Stress in individuals is defined as any interference that disturbs a person's healthy mental and physical well- being. It occurs when the body is required to perform beyond its normal range of capabilities.

Symbol is an object, act, event, quality or relationship that serves as a vehicle for conveying meaning and giving a physical shape to the whole perspective.

Synergy. Simply defined, it means that the whole is greater than the sum of its parts. In an interdependent situation, synergy is particularly powerful in dealing with negative forces that work against growth and change.

Values are systems of attitudes according to which events and circumstances are evaluated. Attitudes and values influence our perceptions. Values can be defined as the beliefs of an individual in what is good and what is bad. Values are the nucleus around which attitudes and behaviours are built. (Among the 'true values' of a soldier, 'self-identification' with—indeed an absolute commitment to—the outfit, regiment, battalion or the other unit to which he belongs is the main factor that bonds men who often come from different environments and cultures. Major Gen Strawson-Blackwood's Magazine- Sep' 1975.) This means that a leader should have a clear idea of his follower's value system.

Vision is the ability to see all sides of an issue and to eliminate biases. What is crucial about a vision is not its originality but how easily it can be translated into a realistic and competitive strategy. Achieving grand vision always requires an occasional burst of energy.

Difference between Command and Leadership is the difference between "Go there" and "Follow me".

Prologue

I will always have with me the feeling that I acquired the essence of leadership while training to be *an army officer*". —*Akira Sueno*

Founder and President of Shova Bo eke Japan in *Entrepreneur and Gentleman*

Traditionally, the Indian Army has drawn its recruits from rural stock. Until a few decades ago, it was customary for most people to take their place in the military establishment on the basis of tradition and social convention as it pertained to their families. A scion of an upper class family or the landed gentry would (normally) join the military as an officer. Similarly, boys from the farming and other such sections of the society would be happy to be serving in the military at lower rungs of the hierarchical ladder. The British, to suit their convenience, classified certain segments of our population as "martial" races and preferred to draw soldiers primarily from these categories. This concept suited them and those times. The British did not entrust the command of soldiers to Indian officers till it became absolutely unavoidable and that too, when pressure from Indian leaders built up and was duly compounded by the Second World War. During the Raj, Indian troops accepted the 'white man' as their natural superior because he was also ruling the country. Today, the soldier is not encumbered with any such notion. Armed forces have moved from labour intensive systems, employing men mostly from the rural countryside with little education, to become technology-driven organisations. Consequently, we all wander in a glittering chromium universe of technological achievements and material profusion-actual and potential. There is, as a consequence, a set of institutional strains, which manifest themselves in a variety of organisational and situational problems. What was good enough for the older generations of officers to be accepted as commanders at various levels is no longer adequate. With the adequately read, professionally competent and worldlywise troops, the ability to lead soldiers and to make them respond to command needs more than those thoroughly engraved do's and don'ts that worked in the past. Now, one has to give that extra bit to the organisation and its people before one gets accepted as a leader who can be blindly followed. Military leaders now have to clarify their personal values and match them against the organisational requirements before hoping to be accepted as such. All this means that today's leader has a far more difficult task than his predecessors could have ever imagined. It is equally true that few modern day leaders have had the time and opportunity to examine their basic personality and to identify their precise nature so that they could find a workable solution well in time. To be accepted as a leader of men one has to expend time, energy and effort to measure up to the demands of these difficult times. There is no room for amateurs in the fourth largest Army in the world.

The behaviour of armies is, in large measure, a product of their leadership and the actions of that leadership in battle. The professional inspirations of the armed forces depend on the quality of the intake, particularly in the officer corps. One factor that virtually guarantees poor performance is bad leadership and its destructive effect on group cohesion. A misplaced emphasis on driving instead of leading leads to a fair proportion of young officers to imagine that there is no need for them to grasp the subtle nuances of leadership, and their rank and status will bring automatic obedience. They do not seem to realise that any leader's success comes more from being trusted than from being feared, from leading rather than driving. This faith in the past and its outdated concept of leadership results in inadequate and inappropriate communication between the leader and the led. This absence of proper and easily comprehensible communication has created situations where there have even been instances of physical violence, including use of firearms against their own officers by apparently frustrated Other Ranks (ORs) in certain regiments. Unfortunately, in some of these cases the victims of this violent resentment were those officers who were virtually born in the concerned battalions. In that, their fathers and before them their grandfathers had either served in or commanded these units. As to what brought about this unpleasant situation and what could we do to rectify it, needs a critical analysis. The systems that created a special bond between the leader and the led seem to have lost much of their relevance when our value system itself has taken a shift towards materialism. That is where the basic problem lies. Could we restore that old time bond between the leader and the led within the framework of today's realities? Both the officers and the men of our army are emotional Indians and it is not a lost cause so far. What we need to appreciate is that there are no easy and quick fix solutions to the requirement of efficient man management and effective leadership in the Army. Blending various organisational demands with the changing times calls for a totally different approach to military leadership.

In this materialistic world, leadership cannot be put in terms of any one predetermined correct way to behave which is guaranteed to get results under all conditions. The environment calls for using skills in influencing subordinates without resorting to direct authority. This, in fact, is a demanding phase of leadership in the difficult times we are passing through. In addition, erosion of traditional values has led to confusion about personal beliefs and values, because one finds that these sometimes do not conform to what one thought to be the "right thing" to do. Kargil has taught us that our junior leaders are as dedicated as they ever were. They led from the front and the casualty ratio tells us that "follow me" was their dictum. That we sustain this spirit is essential. This will ensure that the state of slumber, that tends to creep in because we haven't fought a total war for over thirty years, is taken out of our psyche.

Leadership is not intuitive, but the result of proper training and experience. The peculiar skills required of a leader are universal in the sense that its essence is not affected by changes in time or location. Real leaders of the future are those who have the ability to learn from their own experiences and that of others. All that they need to do is to remain open to continuous learning. It is for the seniors to create an environment that supports and ensure development of their subordinates. It is my contention that organisations do not exist to develop people, but that development of people is critical to their very existence. Let us use the knowledge we have to train our future leaders more effectively. As there cannot be a common solution, every situation will have to be individually analysed based on various principles discussed in the narrative.

How to produce a good leader of men, or how to recognise him, has become one of the most besetting problems of our time. We need to identify and define the problem areas correctly. A time has come when we must sit down and examine the traits and skills that our officers must have before they can come to expect automatic obedience. Traits, which allow an officer to develop into a leader, those will be followed by the led without a murmur.

Introduction

"To be a leader you have to lead human beings with affection."

—JRD Tata

The Indian Army has had a glorious past, has an eventful present and a future that will be guided more by the leadership provided to the soldier and the leader's own beliefs. That the junior officers are top class leaders has been more than amply proved over the years. The 'Kargil' conflict has proved once again (if any proof was required) that our junior leaders have nurtured their traditional values and have lived up to them. A large number of young men, newly commissioned officers, have made the supreme sacrifice in the process. So when, and where, does the system actually fail? We must analyse the subject critically and scientifically.

Everybody joins the military with different strengths and weaknesses. Most prospective leaders with proper training and grooming can shed those weaknesses that restrain an individual, for these are not embedded in stone to be totally beyond correction. These leaders can be taught to highlight their strengths so as to enhance their acceptability in a fast changing organisational climate. Many different theories and explanations of leadership have been developed because of the interest in the subject as a practice and as a research subject. Several attempts have been made to integrate these theories into a workable framework. Unfortunately, such integration tends to become so complex that it is of limited practical value to a young leader who on entering the profession finds that too many factors do not fit his perception. These theories are too multifaceted to validate. But one thing is very clear; no analysis, no cultivation of leadership, can add that magic ingredient which makes men trust, respect, even love a leader. This book on "Leadership" is an effort to draw from some of these theories and present them in a manner where no graphs and charts are necessary to drive home a point.

Military service (and leadership, be it in the military, industry or politics)) is a serious profession. It is not a craft or a typical nine to five job where one need not feel the necessity to bond with his subordinates or peers if he is good at his trade. Military leadership goes beyond that. It is not an art in the sense that it does not require a unique and non-transferable talent. It is not a craft because it is not a mechanical activity. Leadership is a complex skill, requiring both intellectual and vocational training. It can be understood either as the power to drive people, or as influence over people. Some experts feel that leadership is like the weather—something to talk about, but about which not much can be done. Others say leadership ability is mystical—one needs to be born with it. Both these opinions are extreme. One should stop thinking of leadership as something that one person does to another because he is entitled to do so. There is no vocation that is as demanding, and unrelenting with enormous pressures and serious responsibilities as leadership. A man is not born a leader. He must become one. To be accepted as a leader he requires a large number of inputs and virtually a lifelong 'hands on' training. He needs to have passion for his chosen vocation; that is, to be a leader of men. Leaders need to have technical skills, human relation skills and be able to conceptualise.

Life is a matter of individual effort, ability, and achievement. Conceptual abilities are developed fairly early in life and one can only modify a little. But most administrative and interpersonal skills can be learnt. The things that I am going to say are not original thoughts on the subject. These stem from the ideas and practices of many splendid leaders in different walks of life who possessed these skills in abundance. Since the subject has a universal appeal, wherever I felt necessary I have drawn from the experiences (and actions) of some of the greatest military commanders of the world, and from those leaders in industry who have left an indelible footprint in the annals of Industrial Management.

Attempts to "manage" the phenomenon of leadership have been frequent, but seldom successful because the Army is not a civilian organisation with a military mission. Therefore, one would like to concede that; though, sometimes these attempts and efforts have been intellectually stimulating and academically invigorating, they have done no specific good to the organisation. 'Band-aiding' and 'fire fighting' methods have not helped us. Nor have these measures helped in restoring the bond that existed between the leader and the led in the past. For, while dealing with humans there is never anything cut and dried, simple and straightforward.[1] The leader needs to recognise that his professional competence and technical know-how, regardless of how well developed these may be, are in themselves insufficient. Knowledge of people and what makes them tick must be merged with it. Successful leaders in the industry have inspired a lot of literature on the subject of 'leadership'. At places I have drawn from their experiences and included their more famous quotes which sum up their fundamental philosophy on the subject of leadership. This has been done with a view to emphasise the point that basic ingredients are the same, whether you are aspiring to be an industry baron, or a successful commander of men in uniform.

"Is the leader a manager"? This question often figures in various discussions and seminars held at various training institutes. The problem is that no one has as yet figured out how to manage people effectively; they have to be led. For that matter, a military leader is expected to find, fight and finish the nation's enemies. In this endeavour Captain so and so can be ordered to risk his life and to kill; Mr so and so has no such commitment. He can always walk away from this uncomfortable liability and no one will complain. Leadership and management are concepts rooted in fundamentally different assumptions about the nature of our social organisation. These are two distinctive and complementary systems of action. Managers do not necessarily lead, and leaders are not necessarily good managers. ("A leader knows what's best to do. A manager knows merely how best to do it." Ken Adelman, Ambassador to the UN during Ronald Reagan Era.).

The word "leader" stems from the root "leden" which, in turn, implies to travel, or "to show the way". To be a leader, one has to make a difference and facilitate achievement of the organisational goals. Certain traits are necessary for doing this. The subtle differences between leadership and management get discussed in various forums. In fact, the latest research on leadership is generally managerial in focus. It treats leadership as one part of the manager's job. We will discuss different aspects of the issues involved later in the text. Leadership complements management, it does not replace it. Leadership is a characteristic, a relationship between leader and follower rather than an attribute of individuals. One can learn to manage humans but can one also successfully lead them; that is a different ballgame all together. I primarily intend to examine the steps which are required to prepare our officers- especially junior officers- for situations where they can blend both the leadership and managerial skills that are needed today without in any way compromising on their fundamental values. I will attempt to discuss the issue of leader vs. manager, leaving the final judgement to the reader, be it a military leader or a manager from the industry. As we go along it will become clear that the basic traits required are common.

The most important principles of leadership are, perhaps, five in number. First, the need for common ground between the leader and the led; and, the leader's ability to adjust to a complex social environment. This has to be more than merely a joint material incentive or common means to different ends. A leader will require emotional and intellectual maturity for this to happen. Second, for leadership to be seen as a special aspect of management concerned with tuning and using the most valuable of all resources, people. Third, for the leader to make proper use of discipline while ensuring the desired response from his subordinates. This should be in tune with the times, with the nature of the task and deployment of the troops under command. Fourth, for all levels of authority up to the highest level to realise that their authority ultimately stems not from rank or status, but from their identification with and knowledge of the system. And last, there is the catalyst of good communication and an ability to acquire perspective, without which observance of these principles is not possible. Whether our officers are measuring up to these peculiar requirements so as to make troops respond more enthusiastically to the task, unpleasant or otherwise, is the need of the day. This will be discussed at some length. The aforesaid will form the broad framework of this book.

What follows hereafter is only a broad analysis of the issues involved. Eventually a leader has to find his own methods and modalities in order to draw the responses he desires. All that he needs to accept is that leadership, like honour, is hard to identify with precision. Different approaches to leadership are adopted for reasons of personal preference, customs and the nature of the tasks being performed. It will also depend on the background, affiliation, training and feelings of people performing them. I don't expect a reader to take my word on everything covered in this text. What, perhaps, will be accepted are useful tips and guidelines from those wno went on to become great leaders in different walks of life in their lifetime. Fairly large number of quotable quotes from these wise ones have been added for this reason.

Good thing is that 'leadership' can be studied, analysed and planned. It is hoped that some of the skills required and defined hereafter are learnable; otherwise this endeavour has no purpose. A casual glance through the above observations will tell a reader that there is nothing new in this. We are all aware of these basic guidelines. So what purpose will this book serve? A valid question if you ignore the falling standards of inter-personnel relationships, and if you overlook the need for a course correction then yes, this is a wasted effort.

Note:

1. "Leaders must be seen up front, up to date, up to their job, and up early in the morning". Lord Seiff Director Marks & Spencer, England

Contents

Chapter 1

Know and Organise Yourself

"Know the enemy and know yourself; in a hundred battles you will never be in peril. When you are ignorant of the enemy but know yourself, your chances of winning or losing are equal. If ignorant of both yourself and your enemy, you are certain in every battle to be in peril."

—Sun Tzu

"Knowing thyself is the essence of knowledge."

—Socrates

"Know thyself" has been the inscription over the 'ORACLE' software office in Delphi, USA. Knowing one's self is an integral and critically important part of the nature and process of "leadership." Until you truly know yourself, your strengths and weaknesses, know what you want to do and why you want to do it, chances of success are minimal. It is particularly important to know of one's weaknesses, because then you know that you have to do something about them before the subordinates accept you as one who could be trusted with their lives. Knowing one's weakness is power. It allows one to be constantly on guard and alert to a situation. Before one gets on to examine the essentials of 'leadership' in today's environment it is important to take stock of the immediate and intimate perceptions. There are three kinds of circumstances that will keep you from living up to your optimum potential. These are; first, when you allow yourself to be so influenced by others that independent thinking becomes secondary. Second, when you allow somebody else to control your personal and professional life. Third, to be so attached to anything or anyone to such an extent that this attachment starts guiding your actions and judgement. These influences are not just restricted to those that are external to you; these can also come from within as a part of personality traits. Allowing yourself to be controlled by others can lead you to be cut off from the experience of your own uniqueness and specialities in such a manner that you are barely able to stand up even for yourself, standing up for your subordinates then becomes an impossibility. In such a situation, to hope to be accepted as a leader becomes a pipe dream. We have to understand that what a leader needs is the mental attitude so as to be able to exercise effective leadership.

Attachment is equally dangerous for someone wanting to be a leader in his own right. Attachment means being dependent, either on someone or something. It is the result of identifying yourself too strongly with the external environment and other people, who could be your superiors, peers, or subordinates. Attachment colours one's judgement and therefore, restricts a professional approach to people and situations. That is, attachment makes you dependent like an invalid on crutches, or another external support. Whereas influence colours your personality, attachment destroys personality altogether. When one starts growing and maturing in service one finds that the experience of being influenced or controlled by others is usually painful because by then an individual finds that there is no room for initiative, drive and courage, or for standing up to what one perceives to be right. In the case of attachment the damage is subtle, because one is usually not very conscious of it; and therefore, often does not make a deliberate effort to get out of that state. All these factors are restrictive insofar as personal growth and development of an officer, as a leader fit to lead combat soldiers in war or people in any organisation, are concerned. How to get out of this situation and its resultant effects is something that needs to be learnt at a young age.

Fact of the matter is that in spite of a high level of intellectual and professional competence talented people sometimes do not know how to develop themselves. When one is a young subaltern, it is not unusual to be influenced by seniors who one perceives to be 'role models'. That, in a way, is healthy because the influence and actions of that superior can only lead to a better growth. One of the most important catalysts for growth, especially in developing the elusive skills of leadership, is the availability of role models. Exposure to senior-level role models can be good or bad for developing leaders, depending on the attributes of the models. In an environment that disregards how the results are achieved wrong signals could be going to those subordinates who wish to move up the ladder someday. If one thinks about it, learning from a role model is not all that easy—it involves perceptive observations, figuring out which behaviours are the most central, determining which approach fits one's style, and then practicing the new way of performing. The trouble starts when that influence comes from a malcontent or a theorist who in spite of his 'self proclaimed' brilliance and 'assumed' professional competence did not get his due for reasons other than merit. The Army, like any other big organisation, has enough of such characters who talk about changing the whole system because they will not change themselves. Since they do not realise that in any social order they will be misfits in any case, they try to find conviction for their thoughts by finding agreement amongst impressionable youngsters. The organisation cannot always weed out such characters, it is for the individual young officer to identify them and steer away.

Personal Organisation

When I was promoted to the rank of 'captain' and given charge as an officiating company commander I was thrilled no end. I naturally found the job of looking after the training, well-being, and fitness of a hundred odd men to be very exciting and demanding. I would be on parade early morning, checking this thing and that, working like mad throughout the day. Come night time and I still had too many things to do. My head would be full of all that needed doing and things that required further 'fine-tuning'. In short, I was too concerned by matters affecting my command and my own standards of performance. On arriving home my head would be buzzing. I would wake up at night remembering those reports I had forgotten to send to the headquarters or the urgent tasks that were required to be carried out, but had got overlooked because something more important had overtaken the events of the day. I would lie awake in the night waiting for the dawn so that I could rush off to the office and finish the pending or outstanding tasks. This tension made me rise fuzzy and tense the next day. The stress became too much to bear. I found that I was drifting from problems (real or imaginary) to petty issues that had little or no relevance to the situation. I was reacting rather than acting. Clearly, I was out of my depth. The responsibilities and anxieties of command were wearing me out. The lesson that I was to learn was that I needed to augment myself. The heavy responsibilities of leadership, and the time those burdens consume, tend to crowd out introspection. Even at that reasonably young age I was finding myself 'stressed out'.

A well-meaning senior officer, seeing the kind of mess I was getting into, took charge of my situation. And in an unobtrusive way he started guiding me towards better organisation of myself. The diagnosis was really simple enough. "First off", he said, "jobs are never tense, people are." He also said that the effort you put into work depends on how well organised you are, because to be organised helps reduce stress.. That is, I needed to distinguish between activity and effectiveness. That is, I required a "thought plan" and an "action plan". Meaning I had to chart my day's/week's or month's schedule in a manner where priorities could be assigned to various activities. Everyday I was to make a list of the things that needed doing. That is, I was to establish my priorities. (Priorities are an unavoidable consequence of the insufficient resources in terms of time, people, equipment etc., to do all the things that need doing. Establishing priorities means that while the most important things will get first call on resources, and thus will probably be relatively well done, other valid missions will be only partially accomplished, or will be done less satisfactorily, or will be ignored altogether.) Second, I was working too hard because I wouldn't delegate responsibilities out of a feeling of insecurity; I thought that I was on some kind of a trial. This was compelling me to do every-thing myself, however inadequately. This caused a lot of stress and irritation because I was not sure of my 'tolerance level'. During periods of stress, the area that suffers the greatest damage is self-esteem. My morale, to put it rightly, was low. Things were not going the way I would have liked. I only had to find the right way.

In sum total, the theory described to me was that 'Leadership' encompasses four major task areas:

- **Setting Vision:** The leader's unending responsibility is to remove every detour, every barrier, to ensure that vision is first clear, and then real. This ability allows him to see all sides of an issue and to eliminate/neutralise biases that do not conform to his perception of methods of achieving organisational goals[4]. "Leaders are people who inspire with clear vision of how things can be done better. The leader's unending responsibility is to remove every detour, every barrier, to ensure that vision is first clear, and then real"—Jack Welch CEO General Electric.

- **Designing Interdependencies:** Five major "human" problems confront any working organisation. These are:
  - How to integrate personal needs with the organisational goals?
  - How to distribute power and authority?

- How to develop a mechanism capable of reducing intra organisational conflicts?
- How to ensure effective adaptation to changes in the environment?
- How to ensure vitality and growth, and prevent decay?

Answers to the above questions will always provide a solution to the leader whenever he undertakes any task. The solution will relate to the level of command and the nature of assignment. (These aspects have been discussed a little later.)

- **Creating Climate:** The working environment should be such that it creates an immediate sense of belonging. A leader can do that when he is seen as selflessly working towards improving the professional and personal abilities of his subordinates. Give your subordinates as much responsibility as they can handle, and groom them for higher responsibility while they are training. This will create a climate of mutual trust and generate loyalty towards each other and the commander. The dictum is that a good leader is a good teacher. For this a professional attitude is a must. "Men will warm towards a leader when they come to believe that all the energy he stored up by living somewhat within himself is at their service. But when they feel that this is not the case, and that his reserve is simply the outward sign of a spiritual miserliness and concentration on purely personal goals, no amount of restraint will win their favour —Brig. SLA Marshal

- **Establishing Information Systems:** The world is becoming more information-intensive, and decision-making and quick responses are indispensable weapons. Progress reports on the assignment and the effect of the situation on the morale of the subordinates are two essential ingredients that make one a successful leader.

Quoting Jack Welch, my mentor said, "There are three secrets of success—speed, simplicity and self-confidence. Self-confident people are open to good ideas regardless of their source and are willing to share them." "Self-confidence is an essential requirement. If you do not believe in yourself, how can you expect others to?" he summed up. Having broadly identified my problem he (my mentor) recommended that, I was required to identify the activities that I could delegate to others. Besides helping me in reducing my workload, this delegation would also help in training my JCOs (Junior Commissioned Officers), because a JCO also has to be trained and groomed so that he can be a competent leader in his own right. More importantly, the JCO knows how to get things done; he also knows what motivates a particular squad or platoon. He has to be nurtured, aided, respected (in the Indian army a JCO is always addressed as 'Sahib') and given responsibility. I realised that a leader can reduce the need for everything being referred to him, by formulating standard operating procedures where most of the routine activities are concerned. If you have to make too many decisions in handling day to day affairs of your unit or sub unit then either the authority has not been delegated appropriately or the grooming of subordinates has not been given the attention it deserves. I realised that unless a commander trains and trusts others, he will not be able to relieve himself of responsibilities that could very well have been given to those below him. Delegation can buy a leader more working time. It will help you to eliminate, pass on, or at least minimise the time-consuming routine jobs.

I started making a schedule of items that required immediate handling. Next, I listed out those things that were to be completed in a particular timeframe given, in terms of days, weeks or months. This included reports and returns due on specific days or dates. Immediate analysis and progress on all activities, in order to see if any additional effort was required for meeting the deadline, was undertaken. Any activity that was moving smoothly and as per the schedule was to be left alone. I could always monitor those when free. I was also to see if there was a more efficient way to utilise manpower under my command. For example, instead of employing an obviously competent NCO on a routine job, I could put him in charge of a squad. A more important guideline was that early morning (when one is fresh), is the time for tough projects that tax ones capabilities, rather than easy ones. Easy tasks can be put off for the less productive cycle of a workday.

In sum total the lesson was-"Delegation and Time Management" were the most important weapons in a leader's (whatever be his level of command) arsenal, where functional efficiency is concerned. The crux of the lesson was that personal development and growth of a leader is an important input toward success, both in personal and professional life. The qualities of leadership that one must have start with organising oneself in a manner that befits an individual who is responsible for the lives and performance of so many others is of prime importance, besides safeguarding national security. This is essential for achieving goals and objectives of the organisation. To achieve this end one has to know and organise himself in a manner that befits the organisational profile.

Hard work, including physical fitness, isn't a prescription with universal appeal, but it is inescapable in a military leader. A leader in any walk of life, be it government, industry or any other field where one has to compete either with others or with himself, his capacity for sustained hard work under difficult conditions will separate him from the run of the mill types. Chairman of a company could manage his affairs even if he is physically not very fit, an aging politician can also be a competent leader in his own right.. But a military leader, particularly a junior leader, has to be superbly fit for the men to see him as one who could lead them in battle. "For a leader to secure commitment from subordinates in business, "writes Abraham Zaleznik,[5] "he has to demonstrate extraordinary competence or other qualities that subordinates admire. If the leader fails to demonstrate these personal qualities and is not maintained in his role by tradition, the leadership compact begins to disintegrate." As I grew in service, and as more and more challenging assignments came my way, my understanding of these two lessons kept improving. I could see the advantage of delegation and I could feel the easing of 'work pressure' with better time management. Delegation has been discussed elsewhere. Here, we will discuss the other half of the lesson-"Time Management".

Time Management

Harold Taylor, a specialist in 'Time Management' was once conducting a workshop of senior managers. On a table he placed a large, transparent plastic jar with an oversize opening at the neck. He placed a tray of fist-size rocks besides the jar and asked the participants to guess how many of those he could get into the jar. There were several guesses. He then filled the jar to the top with fifteen big rocks. Then he asked the audience if the jar was full. There was a quick agreement that the jar was certainly full. Taylor reached under the table and brought out a pail of gravel. Shaking the jar, he poured a good deal of the gravel into it. He again asked the question: "Is the jar full"

The audience was now a bit doubtful, and a hesitant response was: "It probably isn't!" He then pulled out a bucket of sand and repeated the process. Before he could ask the question, the answer came: "It is still not full!"

Taylor agreed with his audience and went on to pour water over the contents of the jar; filling it to the brim Then he went on to explain the theme of this exercise. "If I hadn't put the rocks in first, probably I wouldn't have been able to get that many in," he said. In the instant case the rocks were the "must do", the gravel was "should do" and the sand signified "can do". Water indicated what all may be done if there is still time to spare.)

Like most leaders you do not have enough time to do everything you set out to do every morning. And in all probability, you know of no one else who does either. When we do not achieve what we had set out to do, there is a feeling of confusion, compromise and even frustration because the higher authority is interested in results and not excuses. The net result is, wasted time, poor or indifferent performance, and increased stress. The fundamental problem is that when we perceive a task to be difficult, inconvenient or unpleasant, we tend to procrastinate. Procrastination is, for whatever reason, a part of the Indian culture. Any of the following reasons are cited in justification:

(a) This is an obvious "fatigue" duty assigned to me; I'll wait until I get into the mood to do it. More often than not, to a young officer most of the assignments appear to be meaningless and are termed as "created work" simply because he is not in the full picture of things.

(b) The completion report is not due for some time, so why bother now. Even as students we tend to put off serious study because the examinations are too far away. *One has to quickly outgrow this culture because events have a habit of overtaking all the plans one makes for attending to tasks assigned.*

(c) Enough clarifications were not sought when the task was assigned to me. I do not know where to start. If I go to the commander now to seek clarification he may think that I am either shirking or "slow on the uptake". *None of these fears are 'generally' valid because your superior is more interested in an appropriate and timely completion of the task. Normally he would be more than happy when you seek clarifications because that tells him that you are serious about meeting the deadline.*

(d) I always work better under pressure, so I don't need to do it right now. (This perhaps is the most dangerous trait and needs to be overcome quickly because one is never too sure of the events in the pipeline and their impact on the work schedule. Pressure tends to build up creating avoidable tension and stress. Often the consequence is shoddy work and lowering of reputation.) *A young officer must, as a rule, ensure that he makes an immediate outline of his line of action and then keep filling the gaps as fresh inputs come in. He can* *then always generate the final output at short notice and the assignment also becomes a 'learning experience'.*

(e) There are many other things waiting for my immediate attention. *Prioritising is the only way out. Depending on the relevance and importance of the task, one can fit the requirement in its proper place.*

(f) The country's war effort is not likely to suffer if I do not prepare and send this particular report by the prescribed 'due date'. *There are too many reports and returns called for by the higher headquarters. Most of them are duplications and even avoidable. The introduction of computers has added another kind of 'paper work', that does not leave a leader with enough time and make sense out of the information in hand. But all this does not mean that a young officer can decide the merit of an input he has to provide.*

(g) So and so (who had been assigned this task earlier) had failed to meet the deadline. The senior who assigned this task must know that the time frame given is unreasonable, so where is the hurry. *A junior has no business to find fault with the time frame assigned for a particular task, for he may not be in on the full picture. However, if there is a genuine reason to seek more time, one can always approach the authority, requesting a revised time frame.*

The list of excuses can be endless, and depending on your work environment, you could add to it, provided you ignore the benefits of drawing your priorities and sticking to them. That way you accomplish more with your time, and what is more important, you are not stressed out. All assignments have their peculiarities, job pressures, tensions and worries. And as one starts going up the ladder, far too many things-often distractions- start taking more and more of ones time. What methodology one adopts for 'time management' will relate to one's functional role.

My personal experience relates to the Army Ordnance Corps. The Commandant of an Ordnance depot is a very busy man, because he runs a combination of a military and civil establishment. Trade unions of different political hues also keep the man occupied with their real or imaginary problems. To compound the situation, if leaders of one union take twenty minutes of the commandant's time, the other party would like to be one up, with at least twenty-five minutes. If one allows these do-gooders any rope, they could keep the boss busy for any length of time. The lessons learnt in the earlier stages now came in handy. Briefly, the system that could help is, before going to bed at night, list out the next day's work schedule in the sequence of relative importance and deal with it accordingly the next day. Ask the Trade Union leaders (there are any number of them in an Ordnance depot, a base workshop or a reasonably big industrial establishment) to see the "administrative officer" in the first instance. They should come to the commandant only when there is a problem that the AO can't resolve. If an individual has a personal problem, he can see his "group commander" and not jump the prescribed channel. One hour every morning can be fixed, when nobody is to disturb you unless there's an "actual" fire in the depot. One can utilise this time to work on important matters that require undisturbed attention. Next, all the telephone calls could be made in one go and answering those that came in when you were working 'on your own'. Thereafter, the day's official mail could be gone through and directions given on a letter it self. If you have to dictate a reply then your PA should know when he is to come with those pending letters for taking 'dictation'.

Now you are ready to receive 'progress reports' from your subordinate officers on the tasks assigned to them. Often these could turn into "brainstorming" sessions and could easily go beyond the time limit that you have set, because some characters have ideas germinating every minute and they have to share them. On such occasions it becomes necessary to tell the concerned officer to put his ideas on paper for review, and then explain the problem and his ideas on the ground when you take a round of his group. More often than not, it will be possible to separate the wheat from the chaff because "paper plan makers" will seldom waste your time for want of 'in-depth' knowledge of the ideas they want to propagate. These rounds (of various groups and branches) you can take by rotation and at least once a week. Then it will be possible to monitor progress at all the workstations. This helps in getting a better grasp of the work situation. It also becomes easier to take decisions because by having established the procedures for monitoring it will be easy to give a sense of security to the subordinate staff. It also reduces the risk of "learning of a fiasco after the event" and it does provide a useful platform for counselling. This arrangement also prevents the subordinates from creating work for you, because if they were to send "inter office notes" then you would be sending replies without in any way changing the material situation on the ground. During these rounds encourage the industrial workers belonging to a particular group, to come forward with their suggestions and problems, if any. Where the combatants are concerned, the commandant can be available to hear them during morning parade or evening games. Depot Commandants are also required to deal with vendors etc., fix a specific time and day of the week when they could come. It is better to see them in a group because usually their problems are common and a commonly applicable decision can be taken.

In an Infantry battalion or an Artillery regiment or even in an industrial establishment, it may not be possible to organise things in the fashion described above. In such cases depending on deployment and other situations a commander can develop his own method of 'time management'. The only operative clause is that he does not create tension and stress, either for himself or his subordinates. One needs to have answers to some simple questions and one's management of time will improve. The questions are: -

- Do I allow others to hang around and waste my time and theirs?

- Am I doing things, which could be done by others?
- Do I fritter away time on insignificant issues?
- Why do I fail to achieve time-bound targets and how often? Was the time frame given to me (or the one I had set for myself) realistic?
- How and why did I decide to use my time this way?

These questions simply seek information. These are not judgmental in nature. Just notice how you spend your time and make your own observations. Gradually and naturally there will be a change in your time management. All that is required is awareness that there is a need for better time utilisation.

Mismanaging time is a losing game. Procrastination, leaving for important presentations and conferences at the last minute, and spending too much time on low-priority tasks can heighten your stress levels. How often do we hear the complaint, "I am overloaded with work," or "I have no time even for my family and friends"? These situations are obvious stress-builders, and can be neutralised by planned 'time management'. Peter Drucker was a consultant to the president of a big bank in America. Every time their meeting would be of ninety minutes. The bank president had issued strict instructions not to put any call through while the meeting was going on. There were two exceptions, the President of the USA and the bank president's wife. According to Drucker 'Time Management' is essentially a matter of self-education and self-discipline.

Stress Management

Experts define stress as 'the tension and pressure that results when an individual views a situation as presenting a demand on his energies that threatens to exceed his/or her capabilities or resources'. The word stress is usually used to describe certain inner pressures, which can also have physiological effects. A man, when under stress, could experience an increase in muscular tension and his breathing could become shallow. In extreme cases of high stress, an individual may even behave erratically, and the quality of his work may deteriorate. It is helpful to recognise that stress is a reaction that occurs when one finds the pressure of a job or assignment building up without any immediate end to the problem in sight. If one trains oneself to accept stress as a stimulant and not a problem, one's chances of overcoming stress-related problems improve considerably. In fact, inadequate challenge, insufficient stimulation and lack of a certain amount of stress can make the job monotonous. This can result in lowering of morale, and can be a de-motivating factor. An ideal situation will be when one has sufficient challenge to stimulate professional achievement alongside a balanced lifestyle. Dr Louis Kaplow of the National Institute of Mental Health, USA, says, " you need stress in your life. Stress adds flavour, challenge and opportunity to an individual's professional life. Stress can, in many cases, have an energising effect, causing those who are prepared and able to do so to rise to the occasion of a stressful situation by rendering an exceptional performance. Stress, properly controlled, can provide important motivation and improve performance of an individual. Training and experience enhance the probability of such a productive response."

Stress is virtually built into a young officer's career from the very beginning. Stress in individuals is also defined as any interference that disturbs a person's healthy mental and physical well-being. It occurs when the body is required to perform beyond its normal range of capabilities, and leaders are often asked to and expected to so perform. In today's army a leader requires a large number of "people" skills, which are not easy to define and compartmentalise, but a feeling that you lack some of those is stressful. What adds to the problem is an inability to delegate, an inability to say "no", and to accept or be given too much responsibility. Naturally, leaders are generally under stress due to reasons beyond their control. Warfare, training, grooming and preparing for the same is an inherently high stress environment. Commanders, at all levels, are constantly worrying about how those in their charge will respond in a crisis, particularly if the wards are untested in an actual confrontation. Will the unit or sub-unit live up to the expectations or will it succumb to the pressures of a 'real life' battle where life or limb could be lost. Those holding "staff assignments" are under pressure for creating, generating, or compiling 'reports and returns' for the commander. The large amount of paper work (particularly computer printouts) now days, in itself could, and it sometimes does, cause high blood pressure and other stress related ailments in incumbents who are overloaded with information, some of which is really meaningless. They tend to suffer from "information distress". Many of these sedentary jobs are so repetitive and undemanding that an officer receives very little job satisfaction. There is a lack of potential for creativity in these assignments. The consequent boredom and lethargy thus induced can be highly stressful and difficult to get over. Glamorising stress in such situations may help you overcome its adverse effects. Stress is built into leadership, as leaders are often caught between trying to satisfy the needs of their subordinates on the one hand, and fulfilling the wishes of their superiors on the other. Stress has a habit of percolating downwards and that could mean avoidable tension all round. Unless it is a healthy stress (like the commanding officer desperately wanting to win the Divisional Sports Trophy), it would be desirable to find ways and means of reducing its impact. Living with stress, knowing how to handle pressure is necessary in today's leader. Stress is an integral part of purposeful corporate endeavour, in fact. The army is a big enough 'Corporate' house capable of causing stress at all levels.

Very rightly certain well-known psychiatrists advices that the 'Goal of Perfection' is a false goal and must be abandoned because a sustained effort to attain such a goal can lead to nervous breakdown. Stress management is simple in theory. It consists of clearly defining and recognising the root conflict or impossibility, ceasing to expect oneself to do the impossible;

then either coping with the reality, or changing the reality. This can involve changing values, assumptions and expectations if these are seemingly unrealistic. We can work to change what can be changed. We can learn to live with what cannot be changed. We can try to develop the wisdom to tell the difference between the two. As one grows in service, one develops intuitions and 'life management' skills. This helps in making one more competent at avoiding stressful situations. However, there are many situations that a leader cannot avoid. This usually happens when there is a conflict between what we would like to happen and what actually happens. In such a situation it will help if one tries to find humour in the emerging circumstances. (At a meeting of the Tata Oil Mills in the early seventies, a faithful but agitated shareholder said, "Sir, the quality of Hamam soap has deteriorated sharply."

- "Who says that?" JRD inquired.
- "My wife, sir, she has been using this soap for several years."
- "If your wife is so discontented she must change the soap she uses."
- "Sir", replied the shareholder, "she won't do that, she will never do that."

• "Then," said JRD, "you must change your wife!" Tension that was building up in the hall suddenly vanished. JRD had a high threshold of endurance, and this may be partly due to his ability to cut any tension he felt through humour.

The most important facet of a good leader is to have a sense of 'humour' as his best friend, philosopher and guide. It helps him in releasing tension and mental fatigue. A touch of humour can absorb a lot of tensions. It will help if one can generate options to improve a situation. There are always more options than those that appear in the first instance. The key to making stress a positive part of your life is learning to deal with it and use it to your advantage. Management gurus recommend the following ways of converting stress into your strength.

(a) Determine which job related duties you like and do them at least once a day. You may not be able to reduce stressful tasks that are obligatory but you will be able to neutralise their impact. Be confident about handling your assignment, but learn to say no to requests and demands if you feel that somebody is just trying to find an easy way out for himself by roping you in.

(b) Allocate blocks of time for concentrating on specific tasks. These slots of productivity will give you a sense of accomplishment, and thus reduce your feeling of helplessness. And if you feel that you have too much to do, delegate some of your tasks to others. Avoid the habit of taking work home with you everynight.

(c) Spend time with people who boost your ego, they are good at listening and can sympathise with your insecurities and stresses. This is particularly important when the hierarchical structure of our army has layers of formalities where it is often not possible to get a feedback on decisions. This can mean bottling up your anxieties, a situation that can be very stressful. Do not respond negatively to personal criticism, particularly if someone close is making any adverse observation, he may want to help you. ("*When, after having studied the officers of your regiment for a long time, you know them all, you will choose among them two special friends in whom you will have recognised virtue, knowledge, and love of truth and order. You will confide in them the important task of speaking freely to you of your faults, and of showing them to you clearly.*" The Will of Marshal de Belle-Isle-a letter addressed to his son on taking over command of a battalion. Please see appendix for the full-translated text of the letter.) Sometimes leaders tend to believe that their authority can only be sustained if they appear to be infallible. They do not admit that they are under stress because of the fear that any such acceptance of reality will undermine their authority. This is a wrong. By admitting that a particular assignment or activity is causing stress one establishes his credentials that he is only human and is subject to normal worries and problems. Do not ignore your problems. Acknowledge them as they are. Learn to talk openly about your emotions and feelings with close friends and confidants. Ask them to let you know when you appear to be stressed.

(d) Develop interests outside of work. Involve yourself in professional extracurricular activities, like writing a paper on leadership, resource management or any subject that you find particularly interesting. Having a hobby allows you an outlet for the 'emotional toxins', which generate stress.

(e) Exercise regularly, play games. To be in a good shape physically helps you feel better emotionally and mentally. If you are posted on 'staff' and the environment is sedentary, break your routine and change the work schedule once in a while.

(f) Set realistic goals for yourself and your subordinates so that you do not feel stressed by too many failures to meet deadlines. If you set very high standards for yourself or your subordinates it may not be always possible to live up to them. These failures to measure up will lead to avoidable stress. A leader must have a clear view of what is needed and what is feasible. This will also avoid generating stress in your subordinates. Take a stroll when you are stressed-it can help restore your perspective. And to avoid stress in subordinates keep them informed about all decisions that may affect them.

(g) Do not keep checking on your subordinates all the time. Once a task has been assigned let them get on with their work. Otherwise, you will be stressed out without any reason. Unless the task assigned has operational implications try to regard mistakes as a part of learning curve.

(h) Bookshops across the globe are full of "HOW TO" books, talking about various facets of management. Adopt only those ideas from these books that are useful in your line of work. Never accept what is merely 'fashionable'.

(i) Everyday newer and newer technologies are getting inducted. When learning about a new technology, start slowly and build confidence as your grasp grows. Some of your subordinates may be able to grasp the subject much more quickly. Accept their professional competence and involve them in your learning cycle. This will boost their morale and self-confidence and your acknowledgement of the fact will at once reduce your stress level on this account.

(j) Try and identify a 'sounding board' within your immediate circle. American Presidents are known to have, either someone from their childhood, or close confidantes with years of intimacy, with whom as President they can share thoughts, plans and worries. This 'alter ego', acting as a sounding board, provides useful inputs to the leader so that he can give necessary shape to his policy. In our military, higher commanders are entitled to select their "immediate staff officers" primarily because they have greater faith and confidence in them and they can use the collective wisdom of the group before taking any major decisions and thus, reduce chances of getting into a stressful situation.

At battalion and lower levels it is important for a commander to have such a group of officers who could provide unbiased advice and opinion on critical matters. The British had created the system of Subedar Majors (SMs), who, having come from ranks and matured in the unit, were available to the commander whenever he needed to feel the pulse of those under him. Over the years and with the rising of new battalions and mixed units etc., the SM seems to have lost much of his hold on the troops. At times he is regarded more of an anachronism. As far as the battalion adjutant or even the second in command is concerned, with all kinds of 'reports and returns' demanding their personal attention, they have been thoroughly anchored to files and paper work. Any officer in such a key appointment has far too many distractions. There are too many inconsequential little things that push themselves ahead of his main job, which is to be a conduit between the commanding officer and others. There is always a ceaseless procession of events and ceremonials and with the tyranny of the telephone, the pressure of circumstances and deadlines, there is virtually no time for him to collect his wits, much less to think and reflect. He cannot possibly provide enough input to his commander. At company and platoon level, where the troops could be occupying pickets spread over wide areas, it is even more difficult for a young major or a captain to keep track of the mental and physical state of his men. The young commanders can encourage participation while planning various activities and actions. This participation allows everyone to overcome stress. *The problem becomes particularly acute when pickets and posts are isolated and often unapproachable due to inclement weather, snowstorms, etc. In such a situation it would be prudent to identify those subordinates who have enough wisdom and common sense to keep everybody engaged in some kind of activity which distracts from boredom and fears generated by loneliness. Physical activities like games and sports will normally not be possible at these altitudes. In such a situation, a company or platoon level 'war game' or any activity that stretches mental faculties could be useful in diverting individual attention. Now that more and more soldiers have a higher level of education one can encourage them to take up 'correspondence courses' offered by various universities. Besides enhancing their academic profile and thus employability, there will be a definite goal to be achieved. This will effectively kill boredom and consequently reduce stress. Religion also plays a major role in soothing nerves and reducing 'environmental stress'. Yoga provides ideal exercises for the purpose. Including Yoga practices in the "Young Officer's" courses will pay rich dividends in due course of time.*

Indeed much of a military unit's preparatory efforts (or for that matter grooming for any position of serious responsibility) are devoted to developing the capacity to perform well under stress. In this a commander who is cool and collected generates confidence in his subordinates. As a management practice, changing commanders periodically has many positive aspects. Not the least of which is, introducing a certain beneficial stress on other members of a unit who now have to establish themselves in the eyes of the new commander, thus countering any tendency to coast on the basis of past successes or reputation. This is what is described as "healthy" stress. The ways in which individuals within the organisation carry out their functions reflect the organisational posture. Rotating young commanders, giving them a frequent change of assignment will enhance their 'interest level' and consequently reduce stress that comes with a 'fixed routine' and isolated location.

Stress is a fact of life-but it need not be a way of life. Largely, the stress we experience is self-generated. Better organisation of one's professional and personal life with suitable deviations and relaxation can reduce the adverse effect of stress.

Power of Concentration

This is an age of distractions. With interruptions of telephones, sudden orders to attend short notice conferences, and other meaningless events that tend to shift the focus, the more serious aspects of leadership are crowded out. Increasingly, the environment is becoming more and more hostile to concentration. Yet in any venture, success depends on concentration, particularly when specialisation is becoming important. Today, more than ever, concentration is essential not only for effectiveness in work but also for the full enjoyment of funs and games. To develop the gift of concentration, you must first of all learn to throw yourself into each job, no matter how distasteful, plunge into it and soon it takes hold of your attention. Psychologists say that "selection and maintenance of aim" (how often is this term used in the Military in an 'operational context'?), where an individual is concerned, means that you keep bringing your mind back again and again to the task in hand. Your competing thoughts will eventually give way to the selected object of attention. In the end you will find yourself able to concentrate at will upon any activity you select. If the task at hand is something you do not like or don't want to do (but you have to) then it may take a little longer to sift through your thoughts on the subject. In a situation like this it might help if the uncomfortable task is undertaken first when one is still fresh and energetic. Or better still, concurrent work on a favourite activity and the unpleasant one can improve your concentration because the monotony thus broken creates an environment for concentration.

An Eye for Detail

Professional thoroughness and an eye for detail always helps a leader. How often do we hear a senior saying that the situation is in safe hands because so and so who is dealing with the subject has an 'eye for detail'. Having this trait implies that you examine a situation from all angles. You consider what all can go wrong and what will be its impact on the end result. You also are conscious of the fact the inputs you provide to some one higher up could have a serious repercussion on the ultimate outcome. Your concern for the final result and your ability to ignore your status as a big gun just because you want to be sure will always make others treat you with respect. The *Economic Times* once published a story about JRD (as told by Mr LK Jha-a top level bureaucrat) when JRD, as chairman of Air India, was travelling with him. Mr Jha noticed that JRD was suddenly missing for the best part of an hour. When JRD returned Jha asked him where had he been? "Oh, I went to see if the toilets are clean, and that everything is as it should be" JRD replied. "But what took you so long?" Jha asked. 'The toilet rolls were not placed properly" JRD said. It turned out that the father of Indian civil aviation had gone to each of the several toilets in the Boeing 747 and personally corrected whatever was wrong. This is the kind of attitude and approach to professional life that defines a real leader.

A former Chief of Air Staff has another story to tell about Tata's penchant for going into details whenever he felt that his opinion on a particular subject could have far-reaching consequences. At one time JRD was tasked by the Government of India to prepare a report giving detailed recommendations on the equipment and expansion of the Indian Air-Force. As per a former Chief of Air Staff (Air Chief Marshal Le Fontaine) that report of Mr Tata was a compulsory reading for all Chiefs of the Indian Air Force.

Sense of Humour &Personal Orientation

When things are not going as smoothly as one would wish them to be going humour releases tension and works as a tonic. Anecdotes help in conveying the message to people in a positive manner. The ability to see humour even in a tight situatio[illegible] great asset. In a new environment it is important to quickly get a feel of the people and the place. A sense of humour will be a big help in this exercise. Like a lubricant it helps the leader to ease tension around himself. A few humorous and lighter vein anecdotes can make long stays in isolated posts and heavy patrolling less dreary. One can lift the morale of troops by narrating some interesting episode. Some regimental messes have "scrap books" where one can find episodes, real or imaginary, drawn from real life situations during the Second World War or even before. Almost all the Regimental' journals, in addition to serious and professional material, carry a "lighter vein" segment as well. This is to tell its readers that life has its non-serious side as well.

Big industrial houses that have their 'in house' magazines carry cartoons and graffiti in addition to other informative matter. "Mr Bobby Kooka, the creator of famous 'Maharaja' logo of Air-India when given the run of the Tata house magazine proceeded to play havoc with the whole Tata organisation by demolishing the ego and assassinating the character of every Tata director, everybody loved it and was happy to be so described", writes JRD Tata.

Pandit Nehru at the height of his popularity had expressed a desire to the famous cartoonist Shanker not to spare him in the "Shanker's Weekly". He even autographed some of more subtle cartoons of his on the request of Mr Shanker. According to JRD, Sardar Patel had an unexpected sense of humour. Writes JRD, "One occasion I will never forget. Having requested for an appointment with the great man, he asked me to join him on his morning walk to which I was happy to agree, until I found that it was to be at 5 a.m., and that he had given the same appointment to three others. As can be imagined, the four of us spent the next hour mainly in pushing one another aside in order to get a few words with the "Iron man" only to be pushed aside in turn. Vallabhbhai was visibly amused by our antics". A large number of officers and men still remember the 'pep talks' the then Chief of Army Staff General (now Field Marshal) Sam Manekshaw gave to the troops in November/December 1971 when war clouds had gathered around us. He had a natural knack of putting even a serious sermon in a language that generated laughter but also drove his message home. Humour is particularly important when forthcoming events are likely to be difficult and demanding.

Humour is an important element of the orientation experience because it underscores a leader's accessibility and humanity. It is particularly useful when a newcomer is trying to get a handle on what makes individuals and organisations tick. A sense of humour almost always plays an important role in the "reality accounting". It is, as one student of human nature observes, the emotional equivalent of a sense of reality, and inoculates the leader against taking himself too seriously. It also helps break tension in stressful situations, and gives the subordinates an easy way to affiliate emotionally with the leader. (Field Marshal Slim mentions in his memoirs of an incident where he was caught up in an enemy shelling while inspecting forward posts in Burma. While he was looking for a trench or another safe place to put himself in, he heard a comment by an Indian jawan from a trench in his native tongue describing the predicament of the Field Marshal and every soldier laughed. Although, the Field Marshal didn't understand a word of what was said, this thrilled him no end. "If the men could retain their sense of humour under heavy enemy fire and could even consider making a joke of their commander's predicament then the morale couldn't be higher", he observed.)— There are any number of instances where a 'wise-crack' has released tension all round. It is said that Lord Kitchner, one of the grimmest commanders ever to serve the British Empire, warmed to the man who made him the butt of a practical joke.

Read Your Men

"The first thing a young officer must do when he joins the Army is to fight a battle, and that battle is for the hearts of his men. If he wins that battle and subsequent similar ones, his men will follow him anywhere". —Field Marshal Bernard L Montgomery.

Your influence on a man can only be skin deep unless you know something about the drives and values that make him unique as an individual. There have been very few great leaders who were not knowledgeable about the mechanics of this business of 'leadership'. They had a feel of the pulse of men under their command at all times. The leader not only has to believe in his men, and have that belief reciprocated, he has to inspire them to risk (even) their lives for some greater end that they may only dimly perceive. The leader must himself have the courage to demand that they do so. This he can only do if he knows what makes everyone of his subordinates tick.

Certain experts have listed the desired traits that an officer must have before he can expect to be recognised as a leader of men. Here again, management scientists have listed the aspects that influence man management, and in the process, establish one as a leader of men. Five major "human" problems confronting any working organisation are:

- **How to integrate personal needs with the organisational goals?** Motivation requires a meaningful 'motive'. What is meaningful differs from person to person and related circumstances. It begins with being willing to dig deep within. A man simply cannot fulfil his potential if he lacks worthwhile personal goals. He cannot make his optimum contribution to an organisation's goals if he fails to know them and identify his own with them. Self-interest is a prerequisite to motivation because it is entirely an inside job. The decision to do something constructive has to come from within an individual. Ideally, a leader's personal goals, values and feelings are all organisationally centred. A good leader almost always subconsciously makes his own professional growth and development emerge out of a potential and latent reservoir of priorities relating to himself, his objectives, his plans, his team and finally his role as a leader of men in his own right. At no stage does he lose sight of the organisational goals. A point put forward by modern exponents of organisations is to emphasise that work will not be done well unless it is a source of personal satisfaction, rather than a task, demanded impersonally by the next higher level of hierarchy. There must be an integration of personal goals and system goals so that people can exercise responsibility and creativity.

  Fulfilment of personality potential is a valid demand in a democracy and giving direction to this demand is an important factor that makes a soldier respond to his leader. A leader can and should provide the environment, climate or atmosphere that will help him supply motive to his subordinates. What it means is that a commander must know, among other things, that he has a duty to concern himself with the overall physical, professional and moral well-being of his subordinates at all times. In all likelihood, he will be able to motivate his command if he tries to find answers to these requirements. He does not have to take recourse to any managerial gimmicks taught by various management gurus, and somewhat thoughtlessly encouraged by our training institutions. One cannot have subordinates of ones choice. There will always be those you do not like, and those who do not like you. There has to be no particular reason for this. But to succeed in any profession you have to live and work with them. So make the best use of those available by developing people under you. Adaptation to changing environments and conditions requires a realistic approach to life and people. Let this be every leader's mission. JRD Tata, the doyen of Indian industry, used to say, "If I have any merit, it is getting on with individuals according to their ways and characteristics. At times it involves suppressing yourself. It is painful but necessary,".

- **How to distribute power and authority?** These are the basic mediums that inspire individuals to perform at a high level at all times. The leader must be able to distinguish between power and authority. He should know that power only means strength or some kind of force to exercise control over others. Authority on the other hand implies a power that is accepted as legitimate by the subordinates. The only problem is that in a structure where the seniority of a person generally guides the level of authority that can be assigned to him, it can be difficult for leader to ignore his claim for power and authority. In such a situation and in order to retain organisational harmony it might not be a bad idea to organise a team where the subordinates participate equally for carrying out the delegated task. Co-operative functioning can help the leader achieve his aim. In order to practise delegation with any degree of proficiency, a leader must acquire and constantly update an in depth knowledge of his subordinates - their strengths and weaknesses. Knowledge of their 'off-duty' lifestyles, their domestic situations, personal foibles, troubles and hang-ups will help a commander in deciding on the level of responsibility a subordinate is mentally equipped and is ready for. It is not implied that the higher commander start snooping on his subordinates - far from it. The principle is that once a leader gets involved in the day-to-day life of his subordinates, sooner rather than later, he will have answers to all the questions.

"Getting great talent, giving them all the support in the world, and letting them run is the whole management philosophy of GE." —Jack Welch

- **How to develop a mechanism capable of reducing intra organisational conflicts?** The problem could be work or attitude related. In addition to personal adjustments required, there always will be divergent or conflicting group relations that arise and have to be taken into account in any unit or sub unit. The modular or task group structures of the military are, of necessity, based on the principle of teamwork. Squads, platoons or even teams of lesser strength carry out most of the operational tasks. It will be necessary to ensure that no intense rivalry is allowed to grow because such a thing can have serious repercussions. Setting up an individual soldier against the other with a view to enhance performance can be counter-productive if a leader (particularly a junior leader) is not careful in assigning tasks and constantly monitoring its execution. He should never be seen to be playing favourites. Officers who can combine efficiency and fairness with the obvious qualities of a gentleman will receive from their men a devoted loyalty, (more than which) one might say no human being deserves from another. A leader must guide himself according to the realities of a situation.
- **How to ensure effective adaptation to environmental changes?** Often the desire to make changes come over those who work well away from the places where things are actually happening. I have seen that often enough, an individual on getting command of a battalion or a higher formation is in a tearing hurry to put his stamp of authority on the establishment. He tends to bring in drastic changes in different departments; in this he generally tries to undo most of what his predecessors have done, with total disregard to the impact

of such changes on the organisational efficiency. What is worse, these changes are frequently instigated by those who are attempting to make their own reputations rather than generate any real improvement. It is, therefore, important to carefully study all the nuances before making any major change in a functional environment. What can really help a leader is to gradually introduce changes in those work locations that seem to be either slowing down the unit's activities, or where the old methods of doing things have obviously lost their relevance. The Quality Circle concept (discussed elsewhere) can be a big help in this; for, the subordinates may themselves come to the conclusion that their efficiency is retarded because of their old methods of doing things. What needs to be remembered is an age-old dictum, "If a change is not absolutely necessary, it is absolutely necessary not to change".

- **How to assure vitality and growth and prevent decay?** The problem is that, more difficult than getting a new idea into a military mind is getting the old one out. One of the major problems of leadership in the Army is the generation gap-not of personnel, but of technology. Most of our senior commanders grew up with, and think in terms of technologies far less sophisticated than those which they command. This creates a situation full of uncertainties (and therefore stress) where the higher commander is concerned. Social scientists are usually critical of any system where a complete fusion of profession and the organisation is maintained as a closed circle. This tendency perpetuates an environment where new thoughts and ideas, from outside or from within the organisation, are not encouraged. This effectively puts the organisation or the unit into a rut and little or no professional growth comes about; something absolutely essential for development. Initially when computers came into service there were any number of combat commanders who felt that an infantryman has nothing to do with high technology. This attitude was not based on any valid data or rationale. While serving with the Additional Directorate General of

Systems, I found officers from combat arms, particularly the Infantry, are as competent at handling technology as anybody else. Commanders who had held on to their views vis-à-vis computers were rather slow to accept the power of this technology where things like "war games" and "decision making" could be conducted with precision, giving them options that human minds would take too long to think of in the normal course. Therefore, to shed the inhibitions which restrict the growth and vitality of a military mind and body must be on every commander's immediate agenda.

So much of today's leadership literature focuses on the importance of being earnest. Indeed, sincerity, consistency and clarity of thought and mind are very big assets in making one an effective leader. But unpredictability can also be useful, especially when dealing with potential enemies. Your unexpected behaviour can push the other fellow towards paranoia , undermining his strategy and sense of security. Experts say that real leader knows when to forget the rules and go by one's instinct. A well-trained and groomed leader, who lives by the prescribed values of his profession, will find that when he has to take decision in a hurry his instinct will almost always guide him towards the right direction.

And lastly, concentration on self-development will help insure wiser use of authority.

Chapter 2

Ethics of Leadership

"It is indeed an observable fact that all leaders of men, whether as political figures, prophets, or soldiers, all those who can get the best out of others, have always identified themselves with high ideals. Followed in their lifetime because they stand for greatness of mind rather than self-interest, they are later remembered less for the usefulness of what they have achieved than the sweep of their endeavours." —Charles de Gaulle

"Ethics" comes from the Greek word "ethos", which means "habit". A careful study of the character of the great leaders of the world will allow us to identify their specific and peculiar qualities and traits that made them different from others. One thing that will be common is the fact that they all had ethics and steel in their soul. What makes people want to follow a particular leader? There has never much of a mystery about it. Lao, a famous Chinese thinker, saw human leadership at its best when it imitated the most harmonious ways of nature, flowing smoothly like a natural stream. Leadership is a personal art- one which must be flexible in its adaptation to men and circumstances, only then can one hope to be a successful leader. To actualise his potential the leader needs to develop certain important skills. People want to be guided by those they respect and by those who have a clear sense of direction. Attempting to define what makes 'the born leader' some experts have stipulated that a fine physique, good looks, command on the spoken words and a commanding presence are tremendous assets. May be they are, but Mahatma Gandhi had none of these and yet, he galvanised an entire nation, and had enough people with the above attributes (and much more) wanting to follow him. What Gandhi had was charisma, courage of conviction, and he had 'Ethics.' Restraint, judgement of the people and events and moderation were hallmarks of his personality. Nobody made him 'Father of the Nation'. He became one because he continuously displayed an honesty of purpose, integrity and loyalty, fearlessness and a willingness to take personal risks for others. There's a lesson here–the mere possession of every favourable physical asset will not make a commanding presence unless allied to the kind of personality which can add that extra dimension which make others want to follow an individual through trying times and situations.

Leaders who have the requisite traits-drive, a desire to lead, self-confidence, honesty (and integrity), knowledge-based ability and a high level of professional competence-have a tremendous advantage over those who are deficient where these traits are concerned. But traits only endow people with potential for leadership. Training, grooming skills and knowledge must be acquired to make one an effective leader of men. Good leadership, dedication, integrity, loyalty to subordinates and perceived competence seem clearly and historically associated with high levels of military cohesion. This finally defines a good officer, a leader who can motivate those placed under him to his plan of action, his line of thought, where men are willing to sacrifice all just because they have faith in their leader. And a good officer is one who realises that his men will follow his judgement if they are convinced that he too is prepared to risk his life in their defence and interest. To develop this faith we need to redefine some of our old traditions and activities in consonance with the changing times. In today's materialistic world there is an ethical confusion all over approaching an epidemic proportions. In these changing times there does not appear to be a single pattern of behaviour that can be practised so as to yield consistently the best organisational performance under all conditions.

In a crisis, where does an individual turn for guidance when he thinks that what he has been asked to do is not what he should be doing. He has only one place to turn to for a hurried answer—his 'soul' or his 'psyche', or his 'conscience'. We have to connect our beliefs with our actions. Personal characteristics are not easily modified, but one can be trained to subordinate personal feelings to "values". Once an individual is 'value driven' his latent leadership qualities emerge, guiding him in the right direction. One should be able to see both distance and depth whenever he has to take any important decision that could have a direct impact on people and/or events. Leadership is about character and moral authority. Character obligates one to live within a framework of guiding principles and values. ("Character is more important than the brain." Lord Wavell). A leader, particularly a junior leader, interprets and crystallises the values and objectives for the benefit of his group. He sets the climate within which these values are converted into working realities. For this he has to integrate the smaller and selfish goals of individuals into larger, more relevant and designated objectives of the organisation he has chosen to join. He is directly concerned with keeping his subordinates' interest and vitality alive. This means that each day, these junior leaders are expected to make difficult military decisions based on values and principles. Often this is difficult to accomplish because emotion, sometimes apparent irrationality and conflicting interests affect one's judgement. These influence a leader's perception of the situation and problems that he faces. These have a direct impact on the decisions a junior leader makes to overcome various situations. In the commercial world one can get away by electing to be inspired by the path chosen by the organisational head. No risk to life and limb is involved even if the path so chosen is not the one that one's conscience recommends. But for a military leader to so compromise on his principles and ethics could lead to dangerous and damaging consequences. To be guided by 'ethics', values and culture will be the safest and most honourable way of doing things in any given environment and situation. (During the height of apartheid in South Africa when a 'Rebel Tour' of the most well known cricketers was being organised to that country Ian Botham of England, a current heart-throb in the cricketing world at the time, refused to be induced by unimaginable remuneration to be paid to him. "With what face will I look in the eyes of Vivian Richards if I go to South Africa", was his refrain.) Now that is what it means to live by certain principles and ethics. No inducement, no likelihood of personal monetary or professional gain should blind one to the necessity of living within the framework of guiding principles and the ethics one is expected to have when aspiring to be different from the run of the mill type.

When just about everything is acceptable so long as one can advance his own self or can satisfy needs of a superior it will never be easy to make clear moral choices. There will always be competing claims on an individual's ethics, values and principles. One has to differentiate between these three, analyse, adopt and arrive at a decision which is morally right. Principles are not values, because they always have natural consequences emerging from them. If their (junior leaders') personal values are insufficiently clarified, they will lack a firm foundation for their judgements and may even be perceived as weak. Background and education only matter in-sofar as they fit a man to play his part in the structure of a unit. The young officers of today are equipped with a better education. They understand that education illuminates values. Personal value systems set the limits of determination of what is, and what is not ethical behaviour. It allows a young leader to put things in the right perspective. Perspective demands broad vision. What is normally not taken note of is the fact that mental backbone and moral courage go deeper than the intellect. Integrity is of much greater importance than an analytical ability. It does not lend itself to compromise. It is not grey; it is either all black or all white. It must not be worn on one's sleeve but must be a way of life. The leader, be he a platoon, company or even the highest commander, has an implicit responsibility towards integrity and in ensuring that those under his command do not have to compromise on this principle. Every leader and in any field of activity has to live by a set of values defined as "Core Values". Core values are those deeply ingrained principles that guide all our actions. These are inherent and sacrosanct, never to be compromised either for convenience or short term gains. Core values, however, cannot take the place of moral reasoning. It is for the seniors to embed those essentials in their subordinates that go on to develop them into effective, efficient and upright leaders. One first has to learn to be a man of honour and to apply oneself in his work with all his energy and natural behaviour. In this, even if your efficiency is not very high, your faith, your sincerity, perseverance will ensure that your effort is recognised and rewarded.

To be a successful leader today the prescribed values are, effectiveness, realising the potential of your subordinates and developing openness to innovation. This implies that the highest of values pertain to attitude-towards events and towards people. Successful leaders operate effectively because of their knowledge, both of organisational requirements and how the human elements in their organisations may be combined, balanced, and directed toward the ultimate objective. The interpretation of the results of leadership research in the military, and the conduct of leadership training can easily be simplified. All that is required is an acceptance of the convention that leadership refers to the interpersonal process in social groups, through which some individuals assist or direct the group towards the completion of group goals. It is more useful to view leadership as a process of adaptation to changing conditions, which require the skills to assess situations and to provide appropriate actions based on the predictions of consequences.

Loyalty to Subordinates

The commander must show by his behaviour that the "old man" is always on the job. That he sees that rations come up in time, that the mail is delivered quickly, and that he is always looking for better conditions so as to improve the lot of his men. If on all sides there is this common tie of service—of the commander serving his men, of the men serving commander—that will be a unit truly formidable in battle. A reflective reading of history will show that no man ever rose to military greatness who could not convince his troops that he put them first, above all.

One vital requirement of leadership is loyalty to subordinates. General Ridgeway of the US Army once said, "Loyalty that comes from the top down is just as vital as the loyalty that comes from the bottom up". Loyalty is not compelled; it is inspired. Loyalty is a spiritual strength. Where loyalty exists, obedience to orders is characterised by a certain kind of superior-subordinate relationship. If a commander can inspire trust, he will at the same time inspire loyalty. A potential leader cannot demand the unswerving loyalty of his followers unless he is willing to return it. If he sees his men only as instruments to further his own career, he is not going to be very successful. Mutual trust and faith have to be restored if the military is to function smoothly. The cornerstone is 'trust', for without it there cannot be any confidence among the members of the military community. Personal integrity generates trust, and the lack of it can undermine almost any other effort one makes to win the loyalty of ones subordinates. Leaders must dedicate themselves to maintaining the integrity of trust within the unit. It takes only one faithless act to destroy trust and a monumental effort to re-instil it. All experts on leadership and management preach that loyalty is a two-way street, unhappily it is less often practised.

An officer has two main duties where winning the loyalty of subordinates is concerned. The first is to think. The second is to impose his personality and his will on his command, whatever levels of command that may be. He should be able to do so to such an extent that his subordinates put the results of his thoughts (and plans) into action with immediate and unquestioning confidence. He will only become accustomed to think if he finds that he is given a reasonable opportunity to follow the course to which his thoughts have led him. His men will only have unquestioning confidence in him if they know him to be one who spends time and effort to win their loyalty and faith in his ability. For this to happen a junior must be given some freedom to develop his own technique of leadership.

A great majority of leaders tend to focus only downwards. They are occupied with efforts rather than results. They worry over what the Army and their superiors 'owe' them and should do for them. And above all, they are conscious of the authority they should have. Military structure cannot afford a 'leader' who works only for self-advancement, who provides only the favourable answer, or disguises poor performance with excuses and statistics. Managers, particularly in Public Sector Undertakings may (generally), get away with this kind of approach. Where the military is concerned, the whole structure of discipline and *esprit de corps* will collapse if officers cannot see beyond their own wants and aspirations. ("A different habit, with worse effect, was the way that ambitious officers, when they came in sight of promotion to the general's list, would decide that they would bottle up their thoughts and ideas, as a safety precaution, until they reached the top and could put these ideas into practice. Unfortunately, the usual result, after years of such self-repression for the sake of ambition, was that when the bottle was eventually uncorked the contents had evaporated".- BH Liddell Hart). It is a strange anomaly that officers who are willing to risk and sacrifice their lives in combat are hesitant to risk their military career to correct an abuse in the system, or to stand up for what they perceive to be right. A fairly large number of books giving details of 1962 debacle of the Indian Army exist. One theme runs through most of them. That is, higher commanders did not stand up to their superiors when they knew that in their professional judgement what they were being asked to do was neither a sound military policy, nor a winning strategy. Even when some junior leaders who were to actually lead troops protested against a blatantly impetuous and unprofessional operations order these protests were ignored for reasons other than the merit of the case. ("The expected professional calibre, independence of thought and loyalty to his troops should have given moral courage (to the GOC, 4 Mountain Division) to bluntly refuse to be associated with such a foolhardy action. He did not do so."— *Behind the Scenes,* by Maj. Gen. Joginder Singh—on 1962 debacle). So does it mean that to be a brave combat leader does not guarantee that an officer will have the courage to overcome pressures to behave in a manner that is not in the best interest of the Service. For some commanders, moral decisions come out of a personal evaluation of what is right against what is wrong. More often than not, circumstances tend to modify their perceptions and actions. They do not realise that the soldiers today are discerning members of society. They may not flinch before walking into certain death provided they know that somebody in whose professional competence they have total faith is leading them.

It is important to be a sound leader for the healthy motivation of your soldiers, particularly when the unit is operating in trying circumstances. The only dependable deterrent to dubious behaviour is moral duty, an awareness of consequences of one's actions and attention to right conduct. The meaning here is that leaders should treat people in their units and organisations and those outside it with respect, as ends and not as means for further self advancement. The leader who acts ethically will ultimately succeed.

It is a known fact that the expectation of a higher commander for efficiency will nearly always, probably always, be greater than what the subordinates believe is realistic. Analogously, expectations for comforts, facilities and better things in life will always be more than what is considered adequate. A successful leader integrates consideration for his subordinates and his own goal while carrying out or making plans for the organisation. Obviously, an officer has to make a healthy blend of these apparently divergent requirements. He should be able to stand up and present his subordinates' case whenever he feels that the men under his command deserve to project a viewpoint through him. How do these junior leaders, who are competent, cope with these conflicting demands? Research suggests that leaders who balance their own 'initiations' do it more expeditiously. They prove to the higher commander that they are loyal to the organisation and are responsible individuals by transmitting a fairly large percentage of the demands of the higher commander down the chain. They may make minor modifications or translations to reflect the situation, their local or regimental culture. At the same time, they prove to their subordinates that they are willing and are able to communicate a reasonable number of their demands (if justified) to the higher authority. And if the situation so demands they will stand up on behalf of the subordinates.

Any leader, if he expects his subordinates to be loyal to him, has to become an influential spokesman on their behalf with the higher management. Sometimes it happens that due to lack of adequate experience-and in their exuberance-young officers, in the absence of complete inputs, accept that what the subordinates are conveying is right and merits consideration by the higher commander. Subsequently they find that the circumstances do not permit any change of orders. If this happens it will do tons of good to the organisation if the senior tells the junior officer his reasons for not accepting initiation from below. That officer, in turn, should take his subordinates in confidence and tell them why their requirement did not find favour with the higher commander. In all likelihood the men will accept the compulsions of the situation. (This analogy does not apply to an operational situation, but to normal day-to-day life when the troops are deployed in peace stations or 'field areas'.) The leader has to educate his men, to show them that their individual success lies in the success of the group. Strangely, today the officers seem to be taking the line of least resistance and appeasement. How often does one hear an officer referring to his superiors as "they" when he knows that what he is conveying to men is not what was expected from the higher commander? A leader who is weak will always blame his seniors for orders that subordinates are not expected to like. These officers do not realise that a commander who is viewed as a mere mouthpiece for a higher level of command loses much of his moral authority, and hence, his effectiveness with his subordinates. These officers also do not realise that more often than not, a higher commander judges his juniors by their willingness to disagree and to stand up and say why the superior is not right. Of course, one is expected to have sound reasons and be able to mount a reasoned argument, supported by good analysis and where possible, with facts. It is also not realised that an officer who becomes some kind of sieve, simply passing orders from the top or problems from the bottom, without in anyway contributing his bit is unlikely to have the faith of his subordinates, or for that matter the confidence of his superiors. It will do a junior leader a world of good if he stands up for what is right, regardless of what others think of his stand, and if he does not blame unpleasant orders on "them". The true leader knows all of the standards required by the higher authorities, and he also knows the dispositions, capabilities and characteristics of his team. He is the intermediary who interprets these elements in terms of the end result. The quality of a platoon or a company will be determined by the junior leader's ability to conceive ideas or interpret them, so as to motivate his command to measure up to the requirement. It will do tons of good if we educate our young officers to meet an unknown challenge rather than to prepare them for those challenges that have already been identified.

If you are not loyal to your higher commander, do not expect your subordinates to be loyal to you. The attitude you show towards the orders, policies and directives from the top will be reflected in the attitude of those whom you command. A commander's every action must reflect loyalty to his command. If you think that the orders merit reconsideration by the higher commander, do have the courage of conviction and say so. Courage demonstrated by taking risks on the battlefield and with your boss on behalf of your men is a sure guarantee that your men will repay this concern and consideration when the time comes.

In the First Arab-Israel war in 1948, the fate of Jerusalem depended on the defence of "Kestel". The last order given by the platoon commander on the verge of losing the battle has entered into the folklore of that country: "All privates will retreat, all commanders will cover their withdrawal." The platoon commander was killed in action along with all other commanders except a section commander, but the men escaped. This is the kind of leadership that the country and its soldiers expect from the military leaders, particularly company and platoon commanders whose credo needs to be "follow me"- the ultimate test of loyalty to the subordinates. The soldier will expect his commander to provide the lead, particularly in a tight situation. When that happens, the men automatically get drawn to their leader. "Blind obedience", said Napoleon Bonaparte, "is due only to a superior present on the spot at the moment of action."

" The commander must try, above all, to establish personal and comradely contact with his men, but without giving away an inch of his authority.-Field Marshal Erwin Rommel

A leader should adopt a 'supportive relationship' in which a feeling of genuine common interest in terms of needs, values, aspirations, goals and expectations is built up. This requirement is essential to personal motivation as well. To this end, a junior leader must identify or be guided towards identifying those traits he must display to influence peculiar motivational pulls of every man under his command. More often than not this does not happen. At platoon and company level, an officer moves through with 'production line' speed, intent on a short-range "zero defect" performance of almost trivial proportions. From a young age he seems to be more concerned with his annual confidential report (ACR), rather than opening himself to 'peacetime' mistakes and corrections. Somehow, he is extremely conscious of being caught on a wrong foot by his superiors. There is very little realisation that this kind of approach invariably contributes to the loss of small unit cohesion, thereby adversely affecting the morale lower down. It is perhaps fair to say, that as far as the morale of an Army is concerned, the commanding officers of the battalions and regiments are vital links in the total chain. We must become more and more aware of how important leadership is in boosting morale. The leader is the embodiment of the valued human relationships for which we are willing to offer our energy and even, when needed our lives. The leader must be both a scapegoat and a giant. It is for the commanding officer to ensure that junior leaders are allowed to develop into effective commanders of men. The men to be motivated by these leaders must have faith in their capability to lead. It is for the commander to build into the life of a young officer enough variety of experience; this way he will be training the subordinate for leadership and making him ready for the rough and tough of military life. A commanding officer can contribute tremendously if he sometimes concedes the point made on behalf of the subordinates by their platoon or company commander. This way the men will see their platoon or company commander as a leader in his own right who can take up issues on their behalf. For a lieutenant or a captain it is important to find this acceptance because ultimately he will be leading his platoon or company into an operation.

BH Liddell Hart said more than fifty years ago, "A commander should have understanding of human nature, the knack of smoothing out troubles. He should have the power of winning affection while communicating energy, and the capacity for ruthless determination where required by circumstances. He needs to generate an electrifying current, and to keep a cool head in applying it".[6] Not very different from what Sun Tzu, the 'wise sage' and philosopher, had said thousands of years ago. Putting it in today's language-to fight well and survive hardships, (and to survive the elements when tasked to hold isolated posts) troops must be supplied with the stores needed for effective and efficient conduct of operations. The Indian soldier has always been known to be undemanding, loyal, devoted and hard working. But even the best led and finest soldiers cannot hold on forever and sustain a high level of morale and motivation without proper and adequate supplies. The Indian soldier is brave, he expects military life to be hard, and his needs are very few. He is sincere, honest and has tremendous faith in God. He believes in his leader and the leader's capabilities. Completely cynical about national or political issues, he is nevertheless a dedicated man, immersed in his military tradition. He never shirks, and seldom volunteers. The information revolution has made him more aware of the world. He gets information everyday and he relates it to himself. Officers must train themselves to give deep and thoughtful consideration to external conditions affecting the internal management of their professional life. Only then will it be possible for them to draw the desired response from their subordinates.

In essence, leadership is, to a large extent, about taking initiative and capacity for sustained hard work in performing tasks that go beyond your immediate sphere of activity. Leadership is about inspiring people, encouraging them to reach beyond their perceived capability. For someone to accept you as a role model for this purpose you have to have a strong set of values that induces that kind of confidence and trust in your subordinates. To be a leader a man must gradually develop the necessary values, courage and self-control whereby he can successfully become identified with, but not absorbed by, his organization. "I had learnt before I left school that of many attributes necessary for success two are vital—hard work and absolute integrity. To these two I would now add a third—courage. I mean moral courage, not afraid to say or do what you believe to be right". Field Marshal Bernard L Montgomery.

Values-Checklist

- **Authority:** Should it be respected? Should it be questioned when you feel that what is being done does not conform to your value structure?
- **Age:** Do you value people because of their age, how do your expectations of age affect your behaviour?
- **Enjoyment**: Should life be enjoyed, should your profession be fun, is creativity important to you?
- **Life/Work:** How much of your energy should go into work. How important are your family and friends, how important is your health?
- **Legality:** Should the spirit of the laws always be upheld, should the letter of the law always be upheld?
- **Openness:** How far should you carry being truthful, is it helpful to expose your "weaknesses" to others?
- **Output:** How much should be sacrificed for results, what is your definition of satisfactory performance?
- **Professional Standing:** How much do you respect expertise, how far does academic qualifications affect your evaluation of a person's worth?
- **Participation:** How active are you in involving others, should power and authority be shared?
- **Rewards/Punishment:** What kind of discipline works best, do rewards motivate people?

- **Risk Taking:** How comfortable are you with taking risks? Will you take risks that involve fortunes and lives of others?
- **Support for Others:** How much support should you provide to others, particularly your subordinates when they are struggling to improve their performance, Should people live with consequences of their actions, Is emotional support for others part of your job?

Answers in consonance with your field of 'Leadership', i.e. military or industry will provide an adequate guideline for you to act in a 'value-based' manner.

All leaders should read and ponder daily the ideals, ethics and the values that govern our conduct-for these crystallise the whole concept of leadership.

—Akira Sueno.

Chapter 3

Morale and Motivation

"A good motivated soldier emerges as the decisive factor in war. Weapons are important, but not decisive."

—Mao-Tse-Tung

"The Morale is to the physical as three is to one".

—Napoleon Bonaparte

In any army course, whenever the question of morale and leadership comes up for discussion and the participants are required to list the principles that boost morale in an order of priority, you can take any bet that "motivation" will be fairly high on the agenda. Sadly, it is also true that amongst those who pronounce the term so smoothly on the tongue, very few, however enthusiastic, actually do anything about motivating their subordinates or assessing the level of their morale in a given situation. Even fewer actually do anything to grasp what really motivates their subordinates. Either they are too busy fighting their own day-to-day battles to survive the rat race, or the subordinates have worked out the level of professional competence of their commander and can no longer be taken in by a smooth talking superior. They are no longer enamoured by the glib talk and "talking points" so boringly and routinely circulated by the higher headquarters, desiring that these be read out and explained to all ranks during an 'evening roll call' or the next "sainik sammelan". The obvious aim of this exercise is to ensure that the men are motivated to perform and produce results and their morale remains high regardless of any difficulties. This aim is seldom achieved, because more important for a commander is to get a feel of the pulse of his command and then create an environment where the subordinates are actually ready to listen and act as per the commander's direction. No two sets of circumstances are common, for a generic "hand out" to uplift morale universally or motivate people. Morale is affected by a host of environmental factors, not all of which are controllable by a leader. In the broadest terms, morale is concerned with the way in which people react to the conditions of their existence. It is usually applied to those aspects of life, which are difficult and dangerous and often has military undertones. The Concise Oxford Dictionary defines it as moral condition, especially (of troops) as regards discipline and confidence. What it means is, that there is no earthly use in trying to implement the 'motivation bit' by 'higher headquarters', far removed from the ground realities, if the overall state of troop's morale is at a low ebb.

Too many leaders who see motivation as mere backslapping and pep talks ignore an essential early step. They make little or no effort to study their subordinates' needs. A commander who wants to build morale and motivate his command must ask certain elementary questions: what people believe, what they like, what they hate and what they expect from the organisation in return for their devotion to duty and selfless service. A real leader knows that if he listens long enough people will explain how they can be motivated. The fact of the matter is that you cannot motivate a man[7]. A modern commander has to appreciate that he has to grasp and identify the interrelations of the organisational aims and individual motives. A commander can set up all kinds of activities, but getting soldiers to participate with enthusiasm is another ball game. To motivate a man or a unit to perform at their peak for a sustained length of time, the soldiers should be treated as equal partners and their actions and thinking be guided in the desired direction. A good leader is not one who can lead effectively and efficiently - a good leader is one whom the men would love to follow. The most perfect motivator is the cause. It therefore follows that a leader (a higher commander) must have a vision, an ideal, a common purpose, and an ultimate objective. He should have the strength of will and tenacity of purpose to do whatever is necessary to realise this 'dream'. In order to achieve the assigned goal of his formation he will need to win the support and wholehearted effort of his subordinate commanders. For this to happen, the 'dream' must be sufficiently worthwhile for his subordinates to risk their lives for its achievement. As Lord Slim says, "your job as an officer is to make decisions, to tell people what to do. It is not difficult to tell people what to do, but it is difficult to get it done. When you give an order, you will find there are an awful lot of things that will turn up to oppose it".

Many times there will be genuine difficulties in enforcing a decision. It could be oversights, misunderstandings and misinterpretations or orders are given based on incomplete inputs that make a decision difficult to implement. It is in such a situation that a leader is expected to either review his earlier command or set the pace himself by leading from the front. Where a higher commander is concerned, leadership means convincing one's subordinates to accept objectives and to agree that they are worthwhile; a leader needs to display tenacity and patience while these goals are being reached. A simple truth is that one has to define duties and ensure that every individual knows the 'what, where, when, who, how, and most important, why' of his job. Providing effective leadership requires command and control skills. This, in turn, entails information gathering and its analysis; making decisions, defining control and supervision points and monitoring effectiveness of the resulting action/operation. In all this, apparent optimism and high motivation counts for a lot. Always remember that faith or fear propels motivation. Fear however, could lead to stress, which is a negative factor in itself. Faith, either in oneself or in the leader, on the other hand, is what propels a person to motivate himself. A friendly, supporting and goal-oriented environment automatically motivates an individual.

In many ways, the management of information is at the heart of effective management in a military organisation. The basic management mechanism is a means of sizing up future requirements and events, developing the series of actions needed to prepare for them, allocating available resources. Accessibility of the commander is indispensable to effective communications. Soldiers love to talk, and they love to gossip, and the inspirations and aspirations which spring up in the wake of an accessible and concerned commander do more than carefully devised approaches can ever do to enhance his influence and shape the managerial climate in beneficial ways. But all this must be coupled with developing the confidence in subordinates that they will not be penalised for candour or for reporting bad news. Listening is a command responsibility; notwithstanding the fact that lending an ear to a troubled soldier is often the only kind of support that you can provide.

Golden Rules: Motivation

It has been aptly said that morale is largely a matter of attention to small details, none of which is a "winner" by itself, but collectively they can have a profound influence.[8] It is the mental and emotional condition of an individual or group in terms of enthusiasm, confidence and loyalty. The standard causes of good morale are good food, adequate rest, mail, proper medical care and efficient equipment. Good and caring leadership naturally raises the morale of rank and file. A young leader's attention must be drawn to these factors as soon as he comes under the wings of a commander. He needs to be told that the men may be expected to fight well only when the leader takes care of these elementary needs. In addition to raising their morale, care and consideration given by the commander can help men become members of a contented unit, with confidence in their leader's ability to guide them at all times.

An organisation with a strong esprit de corps (which is another way of saying group loyalty) powerfully influences the conduct of its members. Discipline becomes natural; to do anything selfish becomes unthinkable. When morale and esprit combine with cohesion, the military pay off occurs. Unit pride and the urge to protect comrades help reduce psychological and physiological fears. Morale, then, is the main business of regimental officers, particularly the commanders (at whatever level of command) of major fighting units, because without good morale there can be no success in war. In times of peace, effective training and the fostering of esprit de corps develop good morale. In times of war it manifests itself in the soldier's absolute determination to do his duty to the best of his ability in any kind of adversity. Unless suitably motivated, troops may not put their heart and soul in a mission which is loaded with immense danger. And troops who will not fight cannot win, however sophisticated their weapons, however brilliant the plan of campaign or battle. Motivation and inspiration energises people, not by pushing them in the right direction as "control mechanisms" do, but by satisfying basic human needs for achievement, a sense of belonging, recognition, self-esteem, a feeling of control over one's life, and the ability to live up to one's ideals. The inspiration and motivation that comes from proper leadership can harness the 'will' of the individuals to undertake tasks that may appear impossible otherwise. Let us examine the ten golden rule vs that the experts prescribe for motivating your command.

1. Recognise Individuality

Commanders, in their hurry to get on with the job at hand, usually do not take into account the personalities and feelings of their troops, leading to mechanical and unenthusiastic responses. This happens when we tend to take people for granted, when we ignore their aspirations and their hopes from the organisation and expect blind obedience and total commitment. The bull dozer approach—without a sense of compassion or consideration for the feelings of your subordinates and no tolerance for human error—is the classic mistake of trying to push rather than leading. Every grown up man of average competence expects to be treated as an adult and not as a difficult schoolboy who requires frequent doses of discipline. Never try to break down his personal dignity. His self-esteem and pride have to be respected and cultivated in a manner that induces him to perform better and better. Every man has pride, build on it, do not destroy it. This way you can convert a weakness into strength. The effort a leader puts in to build the self-esteem of his subordinates pays huge dividends when things get rough. Compassion and a caring attitude for your subordinates will always make them fond of their leader. JRD Tata's driver Peter says that if he (JRD) unexpectedly made a lunch date he would come down himself, 22 floors in lift, tell me not to wait and to go and have my lunch. This caring attitude and a respect for the feelings and comfort of even the lowest rung of people under him is what made JRD a legend in his lifetime.

To issue the right order to the right people is not enough. A leader must do it in the right way too, considering the nature and special situation of the individuals. We tend to forget that one cannot lead a platoon, a company, a battalion or a brigade; one must learn to lead individuals. A relationship between a commander and his troops should be characterised by genuine respect, ease of communication and the commander's sensitivity towards his subordinates. Each follower must feel some linkage with the leader. It is only then that he finds the reason to risk his life on his leader's command. It is for the section and platoon commanders to establish the link that binds an individual to his unit or sub unit. *"The skilful general conducts his army just as though he was leading a single man by the hand."*—Sun-Tzu.

Motivating the men ultimately rests with the platoon and company commander and to a certain extent, a level or two higher. It is the platoon and company commanders who rely on direct influencing procedures where action by the troops is concerned. This is more so in these days when our army has been engaged in "low intensity conflicts" and fighting terrorist groups in Assam and J&K. Actions and activities are at section, platoon and company levels. The situation often calls for an ability to improvise solutions in uncertain and changing operational situations; often compounded by political influences, as it happens with a fair amount of regularity in the North East. A leader, particularly a junior leader, should have that inner drive that propels him to a state where he motivates his subordinates to accomplish the mission and urges them to excel and move up in professional life. This can only be done when a commander is able to identify the vibes that motivate everyone in his command. The trouble is, that when we are in a hurry to establish our credentials as leaders of men, and trying to get along with the people we command, it is not unusual to miss the wood for the trees. In an obvious bid to play it safe and be ready for an explanation if things do go wrong, some of these leaders tend to go in for the 'do's and don'ts' given in various text books and for the 'hand outs' dished out liberally during different Army courses.

Leaders, particularly those who are in direct command of troops, need to treat the unit or sub unit as an extended family, a family where every individual has his own standing, own personality, ambitions and values. A soldier expects to remain an individual entity and not just some anonymous number. He must be made to feel that he is performing a useful role in safeguarding the country's interests. It is a leader's job to provide for group cohesion by making the individual soldier feel proud of his group's accomplishments and achievements. No one expects a commanding officer to know the family background and domestic details of every individual. He cannot remember the name of every soldier under his command. But he can surely make an extra effort to know his best shooters, athletes and sportsmen. He can single out those who regularly contribute towards bringing laurels to the unit, and suitably applaud their effort during 'sammelans', etc. He can, and should introduce them to visiting dignitaries. Appropriate awards and recognition cost little but go a long way in building unit and institutional affiliations. In all likelihood, the subordinates will be motivated to do that extra bit that entitles them to a pat on the back from the Commanding Officer (CO). Where junior officers are concerned it will be appropriate to quote Field Marshal Slim, who said that a junior leader must know his men better than their mothers know them.

2. Make subordinates feel important

Human nature is such that we all want to be recognised as individuals with peculiar skills, traits and needs. From the most junior soldiers to the highest commander, everyone has a personality. Consider Albert Einstein's statement, that in an age of large-scale events and organisations (and the Army is a large-scale organisation), the greatest single issue of importance, apart from peace or war, is for an individual to feel that he counts. In other words, make your subordinates believe that they are important. A subordinate may be bright and capable, but the chances of these qualities surfacing remain slim if the commander believes in the Victorian adage that subordinates are lazy, that they crave direction, that they cannot make decisions, that they must be coerced into showing results. Such a leader must get off his high horse. He should stop sitting on an autocratic pedestal if he wants to have today's soldiers take him seriously as a leader of men. Soldiers aren't country cousins or village yokels without the capacity to judge people, forever looking for somebody to tell them what to do and what not to do. "CO Sahib ka hukam hai," and therefore it requires no further clarification is a difficult premise to draw an enthusiastic response for. Times have changed. The problem is that even if the officer may not expect reasoning faculties among his men, and requires blind obedience, he cannot prevent them from reasoning and thinking. An intelligent man wants to know why he is doing things and what for.

The art of leadership encompasses the ability to identify potential leaders amongst your subordinates. Giving them an opportunity to germinate ideas about better performance. The successful leader is one who is able to behave appropriately in any given situation. If direction is in order he is able to direct. If considerable participative freedom is called for, he is able to provide such freedom.

People need to feel part of an overall strategy and feel they have some responsibility and involvement in decisions that affect them. So take opinions and advice from your subordinates in managing affairs. This is what theorists call "participative management." This is particularly important when the task to be performed is likely to be cumbersome, risky and therefore, unpopular. This does not mean that you have to put your decisions to vote or some such thing. Far from it. What is required is for a leader (particularly a junior leader) to identify those subordinates who have more experience and capability. He should consult them about the line of action for the mission in hand, modify his plan where required and get the show on the road. People contribute most willingly when they are shown that their contribution has value. (It never embarrassed me to tell my NCOs that I needed their help and advice about a particularly intricate task assigned to my command. And to tell my JCOs that their experience and expertise in a diverse range of fields was essential for better functioning of my unit or sub unit. This always brought an enthusiastic response and often a much simpler solution to the problem than what I had in my mind.) A junior leader's admittance that he needs their help and advice acts as a tonic to the subordinates. ***"When you know a thing, to hold that you know it; and when you do not know a thing, to allow that you do not know it--this is knowledge". —Confucius.*** A young officer must know that it would be wise to use the experience of his more competent and experienced subordinates. The fear that his subordinates may take their leader to be 'wet behind the ears' is totally misplaced. Tell your subordinates that you are not very clear about what you should be doing next and see what happens. They will just love a senior who is honest enough to admit his ignorance about a particular subject or a situation and their enthusiasm will jump many folds because now they know that they wouldn't be sent on a wild goose chase just because you are in a position to order them around. That you are willing to learn and make use of their experience and expertise is signal enough for them to ensure that you do not fail in accomplishing the designated task.

"It is that last management secret—Discover where the best ideas are, and implement them".—Jack Welch

This kind of situation-where experience counts- often arises for 'platoon and company commanders' when they are relatively new and do not have enough experience of the ground they are operating on. These days so many 'Low Intensity Conflicts' (LICs) and ' in aid to civil authority' actions are going on, that lower level officers are turned over much faster due to various reasons. It becomes all the more important for the commander to ask for the opinion of his subordinates before leading them for a patrol or search operation. This shows that he is concerned about their safety and well-being. The fact of the matter is his approach has conveyed to them that he cares for their well-being and safety; and that he is not going to take chances with their lives just to shield his ignorance or lack of experience. They would do almost anything for him to return this concern.

The present day soldier has a personality of his own, and he has goals and ambitions. With a greater awareness and better education, he is changing like soldiers in any other part of the world. Today the average soldier thinks, he can appreciate things, and he wants to make his own judgement, particularly where his own life is at risk. In the process of assigning tasks to subordinates, particularly those tasks that do not appear to be essential for the furthering of the overall aim, the commander may have to part with information and details to which the subordinate may not be privy in the normal course. Soldiers who understand why an action is necessary and worthy of their sacrifice will fight more fiercely, or work harder towards the organisation's goals and missions. By giving them the bigger picture, you convey to the subordinates how they fit into the overall scheme of things, how important their role or task is for the success of the operation. It is for the commander to sift the details that can be parted with. He will help the organisation considerably if he takes his subordinates into his confidence by giving the 'whys and wherefores' while motivating them to undertake that complicated and seemingly difficult assignment. There is no harm in telling them the reasons for a particular course of action you wish to take.

The average Indian soldier still has modest enough goals in life. But he will not be satisfied if his job consists only of his performing a series of acts like an automaton. He wants variety; he wants challenges to his skill and ingenuity. He wants to be solving some part of the problem in hand; he wants more say in how things are done. He does not easily accept anything and everything without an explanation. Once troops under your command know you to be a leader who shares the 'whys and wherefores', they are going to have added respect for your judgement, and therefore, high morale and motivation. So, it is not a bad idea to tell the soldier why he has been asked to perform a particular task, let him look a bit further along the chain of which he is a link. It has been aptly said, "When a man does not know what harbour he is heading for, no wind is the right wind."

Security of course will be relevant, but a little risk with security is more than repaid by the feeling men get that their leaders have confidence in them, that they belong. This motivates them to make that much extra effort, because now the problem or the requirement has become their obligation to the commander. The capacity for exercising a relatively high degree of imagination, ingenuity and creativity in solving problems is not limited to a few people only. I would not be surprised if the men return such faith by coming out with some original ideas that improve your plan and thus enhance the chances of its success. There are always good NCOs and JCOs who are a cut above the usual. Half the battle (of motivating your command) is won when you have identified them and have decided to make use of their experience and knowledge. To tell them that this is so will bring in a response that will ensure that the leader is not let down, because the onus for success has now shifted to those professionals who have been there much longer than their platoon or company commander. (After specialisation in 'Ammunition Technology' I learnt demolition of unserviceable and dangerous ammunition from my "ammunition technicians" and other subordinates that included those civilian labourers who had been part of demolition teams for years. So was the case when I was tasked to deal with "improvised explosive devices".) Over the years and as I grew in service, finally commanding the largest explosives depot in Asia, I felt no harm in admitting to my junior Ammunition Technical Officers the fact that I imbibed practical knowledge and experience from that level. I wanted these officers to do the same; for, that is what would save lives in due course of time.

" When I have to make a decision I feel I must first make sure that the superior knowledge of my advisers confirms the soundness of my decision; secondly, that they would execute my decision not reluctantly but be convinced about it. I think this policy has paid off."

—JRD Tata.

The lessons of military history are there for all to see. Benevolent paternalism, autocratic methods, permissiveness, none of these has really stood up to the test of time. It is only that touch of affection, accepting that one is not great enough to know everything about everything and willingness to learn from others even if they are your subordinates is what helped individuals become legends in their lifetime. Jack Welch, the famous CEO of GE, says, "Keep learning. Don't be arrogant by assuming that you know it all. Always assume that you can learn something from someone else".

3. Guide rather than order

The military is old fashioned in a paternalistic sense. Our system has always had preponderance towards automatic obedience. A few years ago an order given by an officer, howsoever ridiculous it might seem, was treated as if it had emanated from God. In earlier days soldiers were expected to do what their superior officers told them to do. Those who did question an order or expressed a contrary opinion were strongly objected to by their peers and disliked by the superiors. The concept of 'blind faith' in the commander, in today's world is a (somewhat) doubtful proposition. Bringing a diverse set of people to that state of readiness and to put them to a particular frame of mind where they actually want to do what their commander demands has never been easy. For this to happen, the leader has to display a wide range of qualities and traits over a prolonged duration. The shift from an industrial society to an information society has affected our soldiers. Today's leaders must lead an informed soldier rather than an uninformed one. This challenge is more at the higher levels of command. Despite all the talk of modernity of equipment, installations and even our training methods we continue to hold something back from the men we command in the fond hope of seeing automatic obedience and energetic following of orders. This is on the premise that the men understand what their commander is doing and asking them to do. Now, the soldier, by virtue of his better standards of education and awareness, expects and is entitled to receive an explanation when the order is difficult to comprehend. It intrigues him that his view is very seldom sought on subjects that directly affect him and his well- being. This creates some kind of a conflict situation between the need for authority and the need to give people responsibility and information, be it in the form of a "talk" or informal communication. With a much higher level of education and perception, today's soldier would rather have broad guidelines for carrying out a particular task.

It adds to an individual's esteem and motivation if he is taken into confidence when a particularly difficult or awkward task is required to be performed by him. Unfortunately, quite a few commanders rather than explaining the complexity of a situation retreat to one or other simplistic but appealing model of the leadership role. They hope, wrongly, that they are on the right track while dealing with today's soldiers. Apparently this is not so. The reality of the times does not seem to have dawned that the military has moved far away from labour intensive systems where the recruits required no education or skill before getting enrolled. They normally were unskilled, semi-skilled or skilled in trades like carpentry, boot repair and such like. Now the military is fast becoming technology driven where the intake entails much higher levels of education and professional skills. The days of automatic obedience to orders, particularly incomprehensible orders, are seemingly over. Another reason for this lack of faith in orders is the fact that the intellectual potential of the average soldier is only partially utilised today. If you let your subordinate use his independent and creative thinking in problem solving, his utility and contribution to the organisation increases manifold.

4. Set a good example

The Army imposes a constant obligation to meet the highest standards on its officers. It makes extraordinary demands on every individual. Not for an instant can an officer divest himself of the fact that he is a leader and others are watching his conduct, to take inspiration from. Standards must be established and maintained in all spheres of activity, be it the sports ground, at the club, in civilian clothes or even while travelling by train. In this the leader has to show the way. In my experience, whenever a unit had problems, a close scrutiny revealed that the chain of command had lost the art of correcting the soldiers. Once Michelangelo, the famous painter, painting frescoes in a chapel, was lying on his back on a high scaffold, carefully outlining a figure in a corner of the ceiling. A friend asked him why he took such pains with a figure that would be many feet away from the viewer. "After all," said the friend, "who will know whether it is perfect or not?" "I will", said the artist. That is the attitude of anyone who goes about his work in a professional manner. And, the proper attitude for anyone who is going to lead men in war and other dangerous situations.

A leader who is in the profession of leading men in situations where people could get killed must have a kind of contract with himself. That he will always be exemplary in his personal conduct, no matter what the situation is. More often than not, no one is watching him. But very often his acts and actions in different spheres of activities show him up. He is either a man who strives for perfection in whatever he does, because he knows that sooner or later lives will depend on his judgement; or, he trains himself in a manner that makes him a "role model" for his subordinates to emulate. Simply put, it means that the leader uses personal example and force of character to rally troops behind himself. When events take a critical turn, he can bring order out of a potential chaos. This self-training will inculcate self-confidence, which is necessarily a product of self-discipline. The foundation of self-confidence is knowledge. The more you learn about different subjects, the more you want to know. This is a clear road to success in any endeavour. Many of us never become real professionals, because we think that the pursuit of excellence necessarily includes reaching the topmost rung - and then give up because we can't reach it. We seldom realise that the danger does not lie in failing to reach absolute perfection. It lies in giving up the chase. As an experiment, think of some error that you made and write down everything you learnt from it. Now write down the reasons for that error to have occurred. Add what you will do to ensure that there is no repetition. Only then will you be able to train yourself to be in a position where your subordinates conclude that following your example will be good enough for them to succeed. However, one has to guard against setting impossible standards of perfection, because to strive for that will take away your peace of mind. The sooner we accept that we are less than perfect, the sooner we can get on with our personal and professional goals. Aim for success and not perfection. A real professional builds up within himself an inability to ever turn out a less than thoroughly workman like job. (Those of you who watch cricket matches on the television must have heard Sunil Gavaskar repeatedly saying that Kapil Dev never deliberately sent down a "no ball" even at the "nets". The man couldn't have set all those records if he had not tried to be perfect even while practising. In the process he was also setting an example for others to emulate).

To be a role model a leader must quickly adapt himself to his environment. Social conditions have a direct impact on the behaviour of troops. Change of command can often disturb the surroundings. In such a situation the example set by the commander will give shape to the actions of his subordinates. The manner in which a task is carried out will depend largely on the knowledge and personality of the commander. What kind of an example he sets before his subordinates will give direction to their response. It naturally follows then that to achieve success in his command a leader he must use his authority, professional knowledge and personality in the best possible combination, i.e. put his best foot forward. If you demand much of your men you must be prepared to give in greater amounts. The quality of your command, be it a Division or a platoon, will be determined by your ability to conceive ideas or interpret them, motivate your subordinates, lead them and supervise them. Your personal conduct will always be the barometer of the morale of your command.

5. Show confidence in subordinates

America's master motivator, Zig Ziglar, says that failure is an event, not a person. No man is ever a failure, provided he has an attitude that compels him to view a failure as a lost opportunity in that particular event. Fear of failure is an attitude problem. Commanders should accept that failure is only an accident, and no more. When failure occurs correct your subordinate with simple direct orders. And, do not be sarcastic, certainly not in the presence of others. Seniors must accept that delegation is the process of building up subordinates so that they can understand what responsibility is. Peacetime army environment is characterised by over-ambitious commanders who are over-cautious in their approach, which proves detrimental to the requirements of an operational situation. In this the commanders are also inhibited by the fact that a subjective 'rating system' could easily lead to a personal set back if the subordinate does not actually measure up to the prescribed requirements. It is no accident that the military clings tenaciously to a system whereby a superior may ruin sterling career because of a single adverse rating. Consequently, the system instinctively protects itself by strongly discouraging admission of error, particularly serious error. This inadequacy in the grooming of junior leaders shows up often with tragic consequences, when a critical situation arises during operations. An effective motivator knows that that the fear of failure can destroy creativity and initiative. It is much more effective to have confidence and faith in your subordinates and to let them learn from their mistakes, rather than wanting to replace those who failed initially for whatever reason. When you show him that his failures are going to be stepping stones to his success, and that it is important for you that the subordinate justifies your faith in him, he is going to try that much harder to measure up. Cultivate the attitude that you trust and believe in those under you, and you expect them to try their hardest to succeed, and measure up to the faith that you have reposed in their capability. Most of us like to ensure that the superior who has reposed confidence and faith in our abilities is not let down, and that the faith so reposed is upheld. (In a field study of 130 army officers, Dr. RD Pathak, who is currently Professor of Management at the University of South Pacific, Fiji, and Col. Shyam Lal, a research scholar at the Indian Institute of Management Studies, find an alarming lack of professionalism in the system. It does not allow natural leadership qualities to blossom, both during peace and in war — A study report.)[9]

In order to maximise a subordinate's capacity for self-development it is necessary that he be given the opportunity to exercise his capacity for decision-making. A senior must act only as a 'coach' who instructs, disciplines and motivates his subordinates to optimise their potential. One of the reasons why JRD Tata took the Tata Empire from a Rs. 17 crore when he assumed charge of the Tatas to Rs. 10,000 crore empire was his ability to spot talent, nurture it and then let the people grow on their own. He knew how to distribute power and authority. People like Russi Modi(the legendry head of Tata Steel) and Darbari Seth (of Tata Chemicals who turned around this loss making company) are only two examples of effective and efficient distribution of power and authority. JRD spent a lot of time in building a team of professionals to run the Tata's.

Command and leadership are an art, not a skill or technique that can be circumscribed within rules and rigid regulations. If these were so just about anybody could become a leader: for, all that he had to do was to open his book of "do's and don'ts" and arrive at a solution that was expected to work. The average military mind is more conservative than progressive in its tendencies, we do not 'let go'. Most commanders continue to believe in set rules and protocols. They tend to become prisoners of procedures and past precedents. With this kind of mind-set they can hardly be expected to trust their subordinates with responsibility. As fortune is variable and commanders fixed in their ways, only those leaders will be accepted who are in tune with the times; those who are not will fail. A successful leader has a flexible mind, which can conform, at the proper moment, to a changing situation. The need of the day seems to be, to treat all regulations only as 'guidelines'. Intelligence and native instincts (available in plenty in an average soldier) are far more practical than any bureaucratic edicts. (*"The success of a commander does not arise from following rules or models. It consists in an absolutely new comprehension of the dominant facts of the situation at the time, and all the forces at work. There is no surer road to disaster than to imitate the plans of bygone heroes and fit them to novel situations."* — Sir Winston Churchill.)

The thing to be guarded against is an attitude of superiority; of superior knowledge and rank, when a subordinate is trying to perform and is in the process of getting a proper grasp on his assignment. At times, with a notion to reduce tension one tends to make fun of his apparent inadequacy. Nothing kills the spirit of the follower more than this disdain when his 'honest effort' gets laughed at. Never, never laugh at the mistake (real or imaginary) of a subordinate in the presence of others. It will give a feeling that the officer has abused his position by mocking someone who could not answer back. If you are not careful in respecting the sentiments of your subordinates, you could destroy the all-important channel of mutual trust and respect between yourself and your subordinates. This is particularly so when you are new to a unit and the men are in the process of evaluating your calibre.

6. Encourage Participation

> *"There is among the mass of individuals who carry rifles in war a great amount of ingenuity and efficiency. If men can talk naturally to their officers, the product of their resourcefulness becomes available to all."*
>
> —General Dwight D Eisenhower

Making a decision is exercising judgement, and this is the essence of leadership. Modern warfare is far too complicated for any one individual to have an absolute grasp of all the factors involved. There will always be an angle that has been overlooked.

A commander who listens to his professional advisers and seeks their opinion on technical and other aspects has every reason to hope for success. In today's technology driven army it is more important than ever to do so. Resorting to group deliberations generates enthusiasm in the subordinates, particularly if their role is only supportive. ("I started the practice of having 'Inter Departmental Conference' which met once a month where a large number of Tata executives would discuss and attempt to resolve various problems. Most of the issues had very little to do directly with their individual departments but the exercise gave them a wider sense of involvement."—JRD Tata.) Participation gives immediate subordinates a chance to be a part of the final process where details of a plan are worked out. This also gives them a chance to expand their horizon and develop initiative. It is essential for the leader to have the ability to analyse all the inputs, take into account the opinions of experts, then decide and translate decision into action. A leader, if he calls people for participation, must be prepared to change decisions made earlier, provided the subordinates come up with cogent reasons to do so. For this to happen, a commander must be very clear in his mind about the method he is going to adopt for carrying out the assignment given to his command. The method will vary with the level of command and the situation on the ground. Broadminded tolerance and an ability to see the other man's point of view, need a kind of courage in present day commanders which wasn't really required when the average soldier was a humble and simple village boy. At whatever level of command, one must leverage himself. There should be a close group of selected JCOs and NCOs with whom one can share thoughts and worries about the functioning of one's unit or sub unit. This helps in clearing one's mind on the likely course of action and its consequences. This collective wisdom also provides a proper forum for making and executing plans of action, be it a combat or a service unit. Men who lead must have vision of real possibilities of the future and must share their views with others, particularly with their subordinates. Those who become leaders in the real sense are the people who can transmit their ideas, thoughts and energy to others. That is what being a leader is. Trouble is, this ability to raise one's sights, to get above the struggle, to see beyond triviality, is becoming increasingly rare.

7. Your subordinates should "Want" to do things that you want done

Development of enthusiasm and devotion to duty are essential. These elements are intrinsic to every soldier, but they have to be developed, in the sense that they do not leave a soldier's mind and are present at all times and to a high degree. In sum total, leadership is the ability to secure desirable actions and responses from a group of subordinates voluntarily and without use of coercion. It is that combination of qualities by the possession of which one is able to influence the behaviour of others. It is this quality that enables a leader to build morale, unity and cohesiveness in an organisation, and motivate all towards the decided goals. This is what is termed as "positive leadership". It is not clothed in any complex terms or abstract concepts. Simply defined, it means the kind of direction that assumes that the job can be done, the problem solved, and the negative attitudes overcome. A positive leader trusts himself. He knows what has to be done and does it. He is impatient with people who want only to tell him what the problem is, who simply want to talk about what is wrong. He is generally considered almost abrupt and even abrasive in his insistence upon determining what the end results should be and what should, in fact, be done. The preceding definition straight away brings to mind Field Marshal Montgomery.

- A leader is best when people barely know he exists,
- Not so good when people obey and acclaim him,
- Worse, when they despise him.
- But of a good leader, who talks little,
- When his work done, his aim fulfilled/
- They will say: We did it ourselves.
- Lan-Tzu, Sixth Century B.C.

A complaint one often hears from subordinates is, "I never get any feedback from my commander, except when something goes wrong." A factor of great importance to individual morale, productivity and satisfaction in work and work-relationships is a clear knowledge of what one is expected to do and how well one is doing it, leading from which, how one might do it better and thus qualify for greater responsibility. It is a commander's duty to educate the subordinate with regard to all these aspects. Whereas success may deserve rewards, failure does not necessarily deserve punishment. It is common knowledge that motivation promoted by rewards is more effective in generating commitment, than motivation promoted by any kind of punishment. Positive motivation should be the aim of all leaders. It is much more sensible to ascertain the reasons for failure. One could fail for want of adequate resources, expertise or experience. If the subordinate has learnt valuable lessons from a failure, then it's prudent to allow him to carry on with the task. A commander must be able to accept the honest mistakes of his subordinates, if he wants to develop their initiative and experience. Where required, necessary guidance, additional resources and help can be given. But having continued faith in the subordinate's ability to deliver is essential, both for his morale and your expertise in judging people. You wouldn't have assigned him the task in the first place if you were not confident of his doing it successfully. A commander must be able to underwrite the honest mistakes of his subordinates. That is the only way he can develop their initiative and expertise. ("A leader should be the soul of tact, patience, justice, firmness and charity. No meritorious act of a subordinate should escape his attention or be left to pass without its reward, even if the reward is only a word of approval. Unit or individual accomplishments, particularly in the face of adversity, builds esprit when members are made to feel that their contribution was a major factor in success. Conversely, he should not be blind to a single fault in any subordinate, though, at the same time, he should be quick and unfailing to distinguish error from malice, thoughtlessness from incompetence, and well-meaning shortcomings from heedless or stupid blunders." —Admiral John Paul Jones.

Although, it is sometimes difficult, the most productive path to follow is to "build on strengths, not focus on weaknesses". Effective leaders are aware of the strengths and weaknesses of their subordinates. This awareness enables a leader to capitalise on the strengths and convert weaknesses (unless these come under the heading of moral turpitude) into workable strengths. This means that as a leader you develop increasing proficiency in telling the subordinate what he is capable of and avoid dwelling at any length on what he has not done well. A real leader takes an honest look at both his own and his subordinate's attributes, maximising the strength so as to minimise and correct the weaknesses.

And if you are a subordinate, when your superior confronts you with the mistakes you have made, do not find excuses for them. Instead, just explain what those mistakes have taught you and how they have helped your performance improve. Remember the good old saying, " Some men get to the top by never making a mistake - they never made any decision". Also, you should realise that just doing your job well will not get you awards and rewards. That is simply what is expected of you. Since you cannot assume that your superior commander will notice your good work, you must find ways and means of telling him what you are doing. Demonstrate that you care for your battalion's or your company's performance and its reputation for carrying out assignments with finesse and elan.

8. Role of Rewards and awards in motivation

One must concede that the chance of winning a gallantry award is hardly ever a motivational force in isolation. It can only be a consequence of a highly motivated act of sacrifice and service. That a gallantry award adds to an individual's self-esteem is important, but does it also lead to his social upliftment in the community and to his greater acceptance by the group or unit to which he belongs? Armies all over the world have always used awards and recognition as, perhaps, the greatest motivation factor. Unlike business houses where monetary awards are looked forward to, and often employed as effective means of motivation, the Army has always preferred gallantry awards and medals without much of a financial string attached to it. But an important question is, do these rewards create an internal desire in an individual soldier to be prepared for the ultimate sacrifice for his nation? Essentially we need to motivate our men to that state of readiness, where their entire energy is concentrated towards organisational goals and not towards any likely reward. To satisfy the human desire for recognition is not just an opportunity for a commander; it is a "must". People demand recognition. If they cannot get it one way, many will seek other ways. And that is where 'manipulative' members of the fraternity tend to get an upper hand. One factor for the bad American performance in Vietnam, was the indiscriminate distribution of medals and awards under the (wrong) premise that such a piece of ribbon or paper could motivate a man to lay down his life regardless of his faith in the leadership or the cause. Attempting to bestow "recognition" when the subordinate knows he doesn't deserve it misses the target utterly and can do more harm than good. Therefore, if rewards are used to manipulate subordinates, they are likely to backfire sooner or later. Unfortunately, the quota system for 'peace time' awards seems to generate a feeling of manipulation rather than motivation, and it is time a healthy "value" is restored to these awards.

Promotional opportunities are also vital for the sustained involvement of an individual in the task assigned. These largely determine whether an individual will be motivated to strive for peak performance or whether he will just try to get by and stay out of trouble. It is not necessary that each individual be promoted. No matter what we do, the percentage actually promoted will always be limited. But it is essential that every officer and every man know that there are opportunities for anyone who performs well. It is important that nobody feels that it makes no difference to his future how well he does his present job. I think that the Indian Army's policy of inducting almost half of the officer's cadre from the ranks is a healthy step towards motivating men for a high level of performance in every endeavour. That a plain soldier can rise to the officer rank by sheer merit and dint of hard work is a very big motivating factor. This gives the average soldier a hope that his efforts at self-improvement and consistent hard work will bring him recognition, in the form of grant of 'commission' in the officer rank, in due course of time. There are a fairly large number of such officers, whose motivation level continues to remain high even when they have achieved the first aim of being made into officers. Senior officers who identify such potential officers and take an active interest in their grooming, and in getting them ready for selection always earn the eternal gratitude of these men. It is not necessary that all your potential officers amongst the ORs will get selected. But the very fact that you take that much personal interest in their future will be good enough for them to retain a very high level of morale and be motivated to perform to your level of satisfaction. In addition to raising morale of your subordinates, such an act is gratifying to the commander as well.

Sooner or later the needlepoint structure ensures that almost everybody stops at some stage, a high state of personal motivation towards the organisational goal is then very difficult to ensure. This stoppage in professional advancement causes discontentment and disenchantment. Economic incentives perhaps help to a limited extent. Though even this has been taken away from the military, as the Fifth Pay Commission, in its wisdom has done away with what was known as the "running pay band". That was a good idea, particularly when the rate of attrition in higher military ranks is extremely high when compared with the civilian sector. One often sees some superseded officers venting their wrath on the system that did not respect their talents and capabilities. Some of them quit service while others carry on for domestic reasons, or due to the fact that, for want of any appropriate qualifications, they are not employable in the private sector. Their morale in such circumstances tends to get low. If you put them in a supervisory position, some of them will, apart from their own grievances, dampen the spirit of their subordinates with their constant bickering about the real or imaginary unfairness of the system. No amount of exhortations or pleas will make these people go that extra distance for the sake of the organisation. It will help restore the self-esteem of such officers if the commanding officers assign some apparently important tasks to them. Their professional expertise can be made use of in organising training and planning/ setting exercises. It may also help if the paramilitary forces, or other such government agencies absorb these officers into their ranks. An opportunity to thrive in administrative and paramilitary streams could retain and sustain high morale and motivation. It is quite possible that these agencies shy away from taking "rejects" from the military. To overcome such reservations a 'special entrance examination' could be conducted and those found suitable can be absorbed therein. *In order to sustain a man's or an officer's faith in the diction that his own well-being and prosperity can also be ensured if he continues to strive as higher-to-fore, it will be necessary that, right from the induction stage the philosophy of his life is primed towards the prosperity of the community he has elected to join.*

Continued importance and respect while serving with the unit and employment in the form of a diversified assignment could also help in sustaining the spirit and morale of those who do not make the next grade.

9. Not So Positive Factors-Morale

Various studies on the American debacle in Vietnam have highlighted, that amongst numerous other reasons, upgradation etc., of various army posts was one of the factors that led to poor American performance in that war. In our case, upgradation of posts and upliftment of ranks was found to be a motivational force towards better performance. That perhaps is why, earlier, we went in for "cadre review". However, the rationale, if any behind most of this upgradation continues to be elusive. In fact, what we have done is, that now we are expecting 'Major Generals' to be doing a job so far handled by 'General Majors'. This could hardly be considered a suitable inducement for sustained healthy outputs. Maybe increased responsibility could justify certain specific cases, but generally work has been 'created' to sustain some of these upgradations. An added insult to the cadre review was the denial of legitimate dues in the form of residential telephone etc., to the officers handling upgraded assignments. To an officer appropriately promoted and not upgraded these dual parameters could only cause avoidable humiliation and, maybe, heartburn. It took the military over ten years to remove these anomalies. Similarly, awkward situations have arisen for JCOs and NCOs also. The Army should stop over-organising jobs and assignments, fragmenting them into meaningless tasks that suppress the real capabilities of individuals. That does no good to either morale or motivation of people.

10. Discipline or Punishment as Motivator

The very word "discipline" puts us off because it sounds restrictive and punitive. However, once we understand that discipline is self-caring and not self-castigating we will not cringe at its mention, but cultivate it as a motivational pull.[10]

Military discipline is somewhat different from that in other walks of life. Here, discipline is a tool for providing focus towards a desired direction. Lack of discipline could lead to loss of human lives and failure in operation. When a man enters the Army, he leaves home usually for the first time, and he also leaves behind the inhibitions resulting from his respect for the opinion of his parents, family elders and his peers. When he comes away from these influences and opinions, he savours freedom for the first time. He is apt to slip in morals, neatness and in his basic culture[11] , if he is not promptly guided and brought into the system where discipline is essential. (*"Above all, discipline is, eternally and inevitably, discipline. Discipline is the screws, the nail, the cement, the glue, the nut, the bolt, and the rivet that holds everything tight. Discipline is the wire, the connecting rod, the chain that co-ordinates. Discipline is the oil that makes machines run smooth and fast, and the oil that makes parts slide smooth, as well as the oil that makes the metal bright. They know about discipline here. The principle of discipline here is divinely simple; you lay it on thick and fast, all the time"*. — A letter by an American recruit to his family.) All human beings have an innate resistance to obedience. Discipline removes this resistance and by constant repetition, makes obedience habitual and subconscious. A disciplined soldier will do what he is expected to do even when no one is watching him. Discipline is control from without. High morale demands control from within; self-discipline. (*It is only discipline that enables men to live in a community and yet retain individual liberty...You can have discipline without liberty but you cannot have liberty without discipline... The self-discipline of the strong is the safeguard of the weak.* — Field Marshal Slim.)

Where the standard of discipline is high, the commander will always be sure that the tasks will be performed even when he is absent. In the words of General Patton, "discipline is based on pride in the profession of arms, on meticulous attention to details, and on mutual respect and confidence.

(It) can only be obtained when all officers are so imbued with the sense of their lawful obligation to their men and to their country that they cannot tolerate negligence." An important and useful tool for inculcating the sense of discipline is "peer pressure", because one of the strongest reasons for individuals to behave well and always try to do their best, is to earn the respect of their peers.

Peer pressure and corrective action is known to be the biggest preventive measure where minor infringements are concerned. Loosely defined, it is, influencing someone to think, act and behave in a manner that is not always natural. Rather, it is a forced behaviour, resorted to out of fear of being ostracised or to be one of the boys. Comradeship and "family feeling" in the Army can help to form good characteristics in those who otherwise would drift into undesirable environments and activities that they may regret once sanity returns. A successful leader knows that each individual possesses certain God-given rights of 'self-direction' and self-correction. All that the leader has to do is to channelise those energies in the desired direction. A simple and effective medium is available to him for this purpose. A soldier takes extra precautions to refrain from committing offences because he wants to safeguard the name of his regiment or battalion. However, there may be certain things that are normal back home in his village, but are considered an offence in the military. The individual might be ignorant of the ramifications of his actions. In such situations it is not unusual for an offender to be manhandled by his peers for putting the unit's good name in danger of being sullied because of his indiscretion. The evaluation of an individual by his peers is usually more exacting and more severe than that of his boss. The individual also reacts positively to this evaluation because he understands that there is a need to be accepted by the unit. *("The military levels out the differences between people and standardises them. It teaches the careless to be calm, the slow-witted to be alert, the carefree to be serious and the pompous to be terse."* —Akira Sueno.)

When a young man joins his unit, and if he does not have a military background, the peer pressure becomes a whole new experience. It is also the time for another reality to set in—peer pressure and its manifestations in day-to-day life on and off parade. Most of our officers come from middle and lower middle class backgrounds, with certain basic values. More often than not, it is the first time the individual is away from parental scrutiny. It is good to have individuals appear before a group, to explain where they are in relation to the organisational goals and why they are 'off-course', if they are. While under training, the discipline of the training institute and involvement of instructional staff ensures that this pressure (if it has a negative stance) does not lead to any adverse effect. The training schedule itself is so hectic that there is hardly any time for the peer pressure to exert itself. If the history of the unit is long and glorious, and there are healthy traditions to be adhered to, an individual is usually in safe hands. A young officer knows that his clothes, appearance, sense of humour and ability to deal with situations will be the standards by which he will be assessed. The 'senior subaltern' plays a very important and useful role in "breaking in" a new entrant. So does the SM where other ranks are concerned. Modern management sciences describe it as having a "mentor". (Mentorship is a process by which an individual is guided through a developmental plan designed to rapidly move him to a decision-making level.)

We all make mistakes, mostly genuine errors of judgement, which a higher commander should accept as normal, or part of growing up in service. Unless the offence is grave enough to warrant a 'military punishment', it might be more prudent for the leader to ignore the whole thing and let the 'senior subaltern' take charge of the situation. Peer pressure is a very important and useful tool in the hands of a commanding officer when he sees a youngster slipping in his behaviour and conduct. In fact, it becomes a medium for self-correction, without recourse to the kind of disciplinary action that could ruin a career. In all armies of the world, there are a number of instances where the commanding officers have been able to rein in the exuberance of youth in a constructive manner. More often than not, once wild and reckless individuals have gone on to become extremely capable commanders.

I once read that leaders with families and grown-up children make better divisional and higher commanders because they have more experience of the exuberance of youth and those silly mistakes that one attributes to age. They have grown-up children of their own and they understand it better when a youngster commits some mistake. Such commanders are not likely to ruin the careers of young second lieutenants for bashing a 'government' motorcycle or taking their adventurous spirits too far. Instead they will prefer channelling this energy into something constructive and useful to the organisation. (While younger officers should guard against attacks of retarded judgement, older officers should view such occasional lapses in perspective, remembering their own salad days, when they too were green in judgement. — Major General Aubrey Newman in *Follow Me*.)

Appropriate counselling should be enough. More often than not, a young officer will react warmly and positively to counselling and just the opposite to advice. What is the difference? Advising is telling your subordinate what he should do. Counselling enables him to see what he should do, how and why. It's also important that he feels motivated to use and accept the counselling, as healthy guidance from someone who is more mature and senior. Even that may not be required if the defaulter has realised his mistake and has taken corrective action on his own. It is another situation however, when the prescribed norms of personal and professional conduct are violated either by design or due to lack concern for the system. If a man's behaviour is unusual for him, find out why. There is always a reason. Maybe he hasn't been given leave when a domestic crisis so demanded; or, perhaps he perceives that an unwarranted wrong has been done to him. In such situations the disciplinary action should always be to condition behaviour and not to punish. An application of penalty should always carry with it a constructive element. That is, the negative motivation should be handled in a positive manner.

The educated soldier of today will resent anything that looks like meaningless discipline for discipline's sake, anything he can term as "bull-shit". A standard of discipline is required, based on understanding, sympathy and common sense, and in tune with the changing times. An important aspect of this is that after the disciplinary action has been taken; the leader should attempt to assume a normal attitude towards the concerned defaulter. For, if the leader continues to regard him with suspicion, he may just oblige by providing the trouble expected. It is better to assume that the incident is closed after the penalty has been inflicted, with advice regarding how to alter behaviour in the future. Certainly the disciplined subordinate will be aware that the commander remembers what has happened, and the leader will be interested in seeing if the individual's behaviour has improved. But one should not go about seemingly waiting and hoping for the next offence. This attitude merely antagonises the subordinate and can affect his performance adversely. More often than not, this constant vigil and focus tends to create an environment where the defaulter finds no reason to improve his conduct. That will be bad, both for the individual and the organisation. To focus on weakness is not only foolish it is irresponsible. Therefore, the attitude of a leader should be one of counselling and understanding rather, than 'police and punish'.

Some people argue that doing what is right is somehow contrary to doing what is good for the Army, '*Izzat*' of the unit, etc. Thus another negative factor is having a leader who allows things to slide or hide because he wants to safeguard the 'good name' of his unit. The so-called '*Izzat*' is more important to him than the sense of discipline and soldierly bearings. How often does it happen that we see a junior either ignoring his superior, or not saluting when he comes in his presence, and do nothing about it? Even when brought to the notice of a still higher authority this (ostensibly) deliberate slight to, say, a JCO by another rank, an officer is more likely to condone this misdemeanour for reasons that may defy logic. The defaulter may belong to a 'higher headquarters', or may come from the same village, town or community as the commanding officer. This in spite of the fact that the commanding officer had never shown any inclination to protect or condone flaws in those who claimed proximity.

Tolerance of poor or indifferent performance implies that a person's effort is unimportant. For most men, life is a constant struggle between doing what they know they ought to do, and the temptation to get out of making the effort to do it. We often accept sloppy work, an indifferent approach to the assigned task or a latent discourtesy as inevitable, as the order of the day. We blame it on outside influences, changing times, and decide there is nothing we can do about it. Such viewpoints are naïve, and they tend to bring about the very negative conditions that we complain about. It is the duty of commanders at all levels (particularly higher commanders) to do what they can, to create a positive organisational climate. Commanders who allow lack of discipline to continue tend to consider themselves pragmatic and realistic; but they are doing no good, either to themselves, the offender or the organisation.

One cannot achieve discipline simply by giving orders; discipline is inspired, created and maintained by leadership. At its best, it is instilled and maintained by pride in oneself, in one's unit, in one's profession at its worst, by fear of punishment. To allow a soldier to perform badly, even during training or an exercise and get away with it is really an insult to him. He does not want any pity or a condescending attitude, because these simply add to his own sense of failure. Jomini has said that discipline should be based on conviction and not on fear. It is not based on set rules or formalities. Correcting a person and making him truly disciplined by education is easier and more lasting than by punishing him summarily. The leader should ensure that he does not administer punishment in anger or with a sense of annoyance or irritation, but with full consideration of justice and the judicious application of corrective measures at his disposal. My experience is that one always regrets having followed the first dictates of one's emotions. It is in heeding anger that a commander sometimes compromises his command. One can be exact and just, and be loved at the same time as feared. Severity must be accompanied by kindness, but this should not have the appearance of pretence, it should not only be real but must be seen as such. A good leader should look upon mistakes as a means of understanding his subordinates and as a means of educating them. He needs to be aware of the fact that the mistakes may be due to his own imperfections, or due to his failure to give clear orders. Therefore, it is necessary to ensure that the development of subordinates is not arrested on account of small mistakes and errors. There are a number of instances in all the armies of the world, where brash and rowdy youngsters have calmed down with age and experience, and gone on to become outstanding leaders in their own right. A superior owes it to the organisation to make the strength of everyone of his subordinates as productive as it can be. *"The task of a leader is not to change human beings. Rather, as the Bible tells us in the parable of the talents, the task is to multiply performance capacity of the whole by putting to use whatever strength, whatever health, whatever aspiration there is in individuals."* —Peter Drucker.

It is the responsibility of leaders at all levels to do what they can to build for a positive and successful future and to avoid being sucked into a negative downward spiral. The increasing turbulence and uncertainty of a harsh external environment means that the profession of soldiering demands more and more from the leaders at all levels. If we put in as much time and effort on the matter as its importance warrants, a good deal can be done to bring back the discipline and good old regimental spirit our elders reminisce about. It is important that discipline is maintained and sustained. The yardstick should be the same for all. Only those who have disciplined themselves can expect disciplined performance from others. To be lax in the enforcement of rules and regulations, or to make any attempt to curry favours and be one of the group - just to be known as a nice guy - will do no good, either to the leader or the organisation. This attitude from a leader will be taken as weakness. He may be accepted on the surface but will actually meet with rejection from these very men. That such a leader finds acceptance neither from his superiors, peers or subordinates, and therefore, can in no way motivate his subordinates, is a foregone conclusion.

Chapter 4

Subordinate Development

The relation between officers and men should in no sense be that of superior and inferior or that of master and servant, but rather that of teacher and scholar. In fact, it should partake of the nature of the relation between father and son, to the extent that officers, especially commanding officers, are responsible for the physical, mental and moral welfare, as well as the discipline and military training, of the young men under their command. —(Marine Corps Manual)

"As the War Department moves you up," General Eisenhower once wrote to a young general, "you will find greater and greater need for people upon whom you can depend to take the load off your shoulders. The more you can develop and test these people now, the greater will be your confidence in them when you are compelled to thrust bigger and bigger jobs on them."

Any reading of 'Military History' dealing with the functional style of successful leaders conveys one thing; that is, these leaders spent a lot of time and effort in identifying subordinates who were competent, then cultivating and grooming them. This did a lot of good to the commanders themselves because they then had subordinates who could share their loads. It was also good for the organisation and good for the subordinates because they were in a position to take on bigger and higher responsibility.[12] Peter Drucker, the undisputed 'management guru' puts it this way: "Because an effective leader knows that he, and no one else, is ultimately responsible, he is not afraid of strength in associates and subordinates. Misleaders are; they always go in for purges. But an effective leader wants strong associates; he encourages them. Because he holds himself ultimately responsible for the mistakes of his associates, he also sees the triumphs of his associates and subordinates as his triumphs."

Leadership is a quality that one nurtures with experience and proper guidance. A true leader guides, develops and encourages subordinates to innovate, to think and charter the course for achieving success. To enable junior leaders to function under a situation of extreme stress, it is all the more necessary to train your subordinates, because good organisation, good discipline and intelligence on the part of every individual are called for. If a leader delegates as many important matters as he can, he creates an atmosphere in which people grow. Current Army culture tends to produce leaders at junior levels who are more reactive rather than proactive. This culture also tends to produce conservative commanders because a subordinate's error of judgement is often extremely costly in terms of the career advancement of the commander himself. We often tend to get attached to our role as a higher commander, and with the fear of a subordinate's mistakes reflecting on our own profile, we tend to play safe. No wonder the normal thought process is that "for survival, do it yourself". To be fair, there definitely are certain hazards in the delegation and grooming process. Higher management has to discount certain mistakes if it feels that juniors have to be proactive and innovative in combat. It will be necessary for a commanding officer to allow a youngster to be controlled to a limited extent, and that too, till such time as he is "broken in". Thereafter giving a long rope, with a benign eye to ensure that the fellow does not get carried away, will be good enough. Only by allowing a youngster to make full use of his imagination and initiative, will a commander ever know of his capabilities as a leader. Unless he is allowed to stretch himself beyond his perceived capabilities, a higher commander can never be fully aware of the young leader's potential; nor, for that matter can the young officer become aware of his own strength. Once the tasks have been assigned, the higher commander must not interfere with what his subordinate commanders can do for themselves. His interference should only be confined to a crisis where the subordinate's actions (or lack of action) could jeopardise the whole operation. For this a commander must foster capable followers. ("*The acid test of an officer who aspires to high command is an ability to grasp quickly the essentials of a military problem, to decide rapidly what he will do, to make it quite clear to all concerned what he intends to do. Thereafter he should see that his subordinate commanders get on with the job.*"

—Field Marshal Bernard L Montgomery.)

Unfortunately, today a tendency which is fast finding acceptance is the belief that "I can do it better myself". Not even Napoleon (even if he knew every soldier by name) could command ten thousand men individually, and a part of the reason for his downfall was that he tried to do just that. More opportunities have been killed than errors avoided by answering, " I am not sure he can take that responsibility" or "how do I know he can handle this assignment?" One of the main causes of poor delegation and consequently, inadequate grooming of subordinates, is the fact that most senior leaders, prior to being promoted to their present positions, are not taught the art or encouraged to accept it as a primary feature of professional life. As a result, they are not comfortable with delegation. What is worse and more fearsome is the fact that the responsibility for efficient execution still remains that of the delegator. This is where the fear of failure comes in, and it restrains commanders from entrusting their subordinates with higher responsibility. Or if the deployment and operational situation is such that there is no room for inadequate performance by a unit or sub unit, then the delegation could be counter productive. If the subordinate is not trained well enough, he is not confident if higher responsibility is given to him. The 'I can do it better' syndrome leads to a lowering of functional efficiency in the organisation and unacceptable situations arise. This tendency 'must' ruthlessly be curbed because these junior leaders, who have a right to be groomed, are being denied a chance for self-improvement.

From childhood we are force-fed to believe that we should perform every task ourselves, if we want proper execution of the assignment. From the moment that a baby begins to crawl, it is urged to walk, talk and do things by itself, to not rely on others in fulfilling these activities. Freud was right when he said that the habits inculcated in our youth and formative years influence and even dictate our attitudes in later life. And this is true of the common attitude (a form of inbuilt resistance) to delegation.

The process of delegation has become the source of many management principles that have now been translated into a generally accepted theory. Three of them have universal acceptance. The first holds that assigned shares of responsibility should be accompanied by equal delegation of authority. The second notes that less important responsibilities should be shared while the most important are retained. The third declares that authority should be delegated to the lowest possible echelon at which it can be completely used, although not to a level where it exceeds the capacity of the delegatee. It is also a fact that it sometimes takes longer for a leader to explain and tell someone what to do, than it takes to complete the job personally. The only way, by which leaders can hope to survive the rat race, let alone concentrate on their primary responsibilities, is by practising effective delegation. But there is a catch. Some leaders may assume that once they have delegated work, the subordinate is totally responsible thereafter. This is not so. Delegation does not mean abdication of one's responsibility. Responsibility is accountability. The act of delegation implies:

(a) **Transfer of initiative, responsibility and authority to another for the performance of an agreed to role.** One of the gravest mistakes in human relationships is to underestimate the need of human beings to have a sense of the value of their work. Many commanders give lip service but very few delegate authority in really important matters. And that means, all that they delegate is "fatigue work". What is more important is to ensure that the delegatee does not feel that he is being given responsibility because the delegator has no other option, or that he is being made to do dirty work. In our Army there is a very peculiar form of delegation of certain powers (particularly financial powers). In that, the Quarter Master General of the Army can sanction certain (simple) things, but he has to obtain clearance and concurrence from the ministry. There are many instances of such types of delegation where the bureaucrats retain the real control but the "dog work" is done through the chain of command up to the highest level. This kind of delegation is counter-productive because a QMG or an MGO should not need the final approval of a bureaucrat for a purely administrative action, more so when no extra expenditure to the state is involved.

(b) **The retention by the delegator of the means of exercising overall control and for checking the performance of his subordinates.** Delegate enough authority to get the task done, to allow appropriate initiative and to allow functioning when the leader is out of action for whatever reason. That means, establish structures for temporary assumption of authority under certain circumstances. There can be situations where the realms of authority conflict between subordinates. In such a situation encourage co-operative solving of urgent problems at that level and keep the necessity for stepping in to the minimum. This will help subordinates develop mutual interpersonal skills, and improve their initiative and drive to get things sorted at their level, rather than hoping for the commander to resolve conflict situations at all times.

(c) **The willingness of the delegator to delegate and the willingness of the subordinate to accept the responsibility for the task so assigned.** For this the leader should delegate to those who have or can develop competence, skills and character. Higher commanders should stop meddling, let the chain work, and get out of the hair of someone who is trying to do a job. The effort should be to instil a sense of personal accountability and responsibility. One must have faith. A real leader delegates as many important functions as he can, because that creates a climate in which people grow. Authority and responsibility should be delegated together. This will help develop leadership abilities in subordinates and prepare them for higher responsibilities.

Effective leadership depends upon a leader's ability to supply subordinates with task guidance and incentives to perform, to the extent that these are not provided by normal and established sources. The onus clearly is on the superior officer to train his subordinates for higher responsibilities. It is for him to identify those subordinates who definitely have it in them to take charge of any situation given an opportunity to do so. But we all agree that the span of control of a commander these days-particularly when units and formations are deployed in counter-insurgency operations-is rather big and unwieldy for a single person to control everything. In such a situation it could happen that an unprepared junior leader is saddled with an undeserved and inadequately supervised dose of over-delegation leading to unacceptable slippage in the overall plan of action. It is prudent therefore, for commanders to identify potentially sound subordinates as soon as they come under their wings, and start grooming them for higher responsibility.

It matters little whether this particular weakness of commanders (where delegation is concerned) is founded in solid facts or is just imaginary. The problem basically is that delegation means, "letting go" and for a superior to allocate a portion of his authority to his subordinates entrusting them with various assignments. Most of our systems tend to restrict 'creativity', particularly where subordinates are concerned. Commanders like it to be restricted to a level that is safe and traditional. Anything out of the routine is not acceptable to them. Commanders need to answer a few questions before they conclude that doing things by oneself is safe and sound:

- **Who is responsible for provoking, sustaining and maintaining the interests of the subordinates in their work?** Presently the job market is so tight that even people with high education levels enter Services as "other ranks", with the full knowledge of conditions governing them. After joining up, sometimes they find these conditions irksome and unwelcome in the absence of any logical or easily explainable rationale. This brings in an element of restlessness. This is only natural. So long as an individual wants to make a career in the armed forces, it would be unrealistic to expect him to ignore associated factors. Particularly, when he sees his school and college mates prospering in other walks of life. He sees this as an injustice, particularly when these colleagues are neither more capable nor brilliant. All that they seemingly had was more opportunities and, maybe better family circumstances and luck. This generates a latent or a demonstrative lethargy depending on a particular situation, causing a lowering of morale and de-motivating an individual. More often than not, these talents remain dormant and undiscovered for a very long time. It is for a leader to identify these well-educated individuals and assign them tasks that test their intelligence and capability. The induction of more intricate and advanced technology has created enough avenues for such apparently capable "other ranks". When subordinates know that their effort will not be wasted on unnecessary tasks, that the leader recognises the value and quality of their 'sweat' and is doing his best to meet their need for mental, intellectual and physical stimulation, they will do their best to return this concern. Superior leadership performance occurs when leaders broaden and elevate the interests of their subordinates.

Who is responsible for ensuring that they are fully competent at what they do? The commonest and most difficult form of risk-taking occurs when you have to make a decision about the capabilities of a subordinate to deal with a crisis. There is always a chance that you will make a wrong choice. Unable to accept that situation, some commanders keep hesitating in making up their minds and simply drift. There is no way of knowing in advance that any decision with regard to the capability of a subordinate is right or not. But a second best decision quickly made and vigorously carried out is better than the best decision made too late and half-heartedly carried out. Risk taking is the essential first step in making decisions or accepting responsibility for discovering the potential of your subordinates. This is essential because in times of emergency, a background of risk-taking is our surest safeguard against danger. Under stress (and in war, a commander often is), the leader who has not learnt to take risks with his subordinate's capabilities is panic stricken, because he has never discovered how far he can try his luck without being foolhardy. Give your subordinates a chance to operate, to make honest mistakes, to learn through experience. People who are good do not expect never to make mistakes; but they expect always to learn from their mistakes.

So push decision-making down to the level that is going to handle it. Have faith in your subordinates. This does not mean that a commander is to divest himself of all responsibility. On the contrary, he must continue to check on the progress of the mission. This should be done in a methodical, planned way and not be a frantic checking done by a nervous and insecure boss. This checking would convey to the subordinate that the commander is involved and interested; the matter is serious and important enough for the subordinate to complete well in time. In a technology-oriented military it is no longer possible to have only simple problems with simple solutions.

A lot of innovation, quick thinking and mastery over a wide range of skills are the need of the day. Your subordinates can develop these skills only when they are given a chance to make "peace time" mistakes. Clearly, the higher commanders in the chain of command are required to ensure that the subordinates are trained to accept responsibilities beyond their present status. For this there is a need for deliberate action so that everybody down the chain gets trained. My experience is that commanders who fear youth and inexperience are too often wrong. More of our mistakes come from fixed convictions rather than from taking a chance. George Armstrong Custer was a Brigade commander during the American Civil War at the age of 23. Azim Premji was not even thirty when destiny placed him at the head of WIPRO, then into making soaps and oil. He had the vision and confidence in his ability to shift focus of the company into newer fields. Today he controls one of the largest and richest computer empires in India. What has been the secret of his success? Simple. "Think big. Never compromise on fundamental values. Look ahead, be self confident and have the best around you. Be committed to quality and play to win," says he. There are any number of young men and women in the industrial field who have made a mark for themselves and for the business empire they head, either by default or by design. What has helped them is the fact that their elders or seniors gave them a basic vision, a set of values, an attitude to succeed and then freedom of action. Stimulation, challenge and enough freedom to develop his own resourcefulness allows a junior leader to grow into a confident commander who can handle just about any situation. It is for the seniors to give a chance to the juniors to develop the vision that makes them leaders in their own right.

Effective leaders learn how to do, what they do by doing it, by watching others try to do and, sometimes, by messing the whole thing up. If we want to train our junior officers as leaders of men, then commanders at all levels must reconcile to the need for assigning the job to someone else and accepting a performance which will be "good enough". A true leader creates an environment in which people continually learn and grow. I know of a commander who had a system, where on a particular day in a week, the JCOs assumed the responsibility of running his headquarters, with only a captain on duty to ensure smooth functioning (as per regulations only an officer can perform certain tasks). The commander never had an occasion to regret his decision. Similarly a battalion commander, while on active duty in an operational area, used to pull out his company commanders unannounced. Second in commands were expected to handle the forward posts for an undefined duration in the absence of the regular incumbents. His brigade commander was not very happy with this unorthodox method of training, but nothing untoward happened for him to call for suspension of this method of delegation and 'subordinate training'. The battalion commander could actually boast that any officer or JCO in his battalion could handle any assignment on a short notice. That the battalion did extremely well during operations in spite of heavy 'officer causality' is a matter of record. Full credit goes to the commander who reposed faith in his subordinates when things were quiet and he had the time to train them for higher responsibility.

- **Who is at fault when it takes an unduly long time for the subordinates to understand and appreciate instructions?** One factor a commander needs to guard against is a tendency to allow the urgency of the task to override common sense, and to delegate the task to someone who has not been prepared for the same. To further compound the situation, some commanders, in case of a failure in such circumstances, tend to 'undeservingly' pass the blame on the subordinate. It is not unusual to come across situations where a leader sees everything as right or wrong, true or false. These leaders are puzzled, baffled and distressed when situations turn out to be neither, with large areas of "grey". They keep expecting the organisation to go back to the "good old days" when everything was clear-cut; you knew exactly what you were supposed to do and were given the wherewithal to do it.

This clearly calls for an 'honest' introspection by the commander. He has to ensure that the task is delegated to the right person, one who has adequate knowledge, experience, training and grooming for the job. He must see that his briefing is complete in every respect, and give sufficient time to the subordinate to assimilate all that has been communicated. Let the subordinate ask questions, however stupid or inconsequential these may sound at the time. More often than not, the commander himself may not know all the answers. In such a situation he earns the respect of his subordinate when he owns up that he does not know, but the two will find an answer jointly as they go along with the assignment. It will earn the subordinate's goodwill and loyalty if the commander also tells him that he expects the delegatee to educate him if he finds the answer to the problem by himself. Here the manner in which a task is delegated assumes importance. First of all, the subordinate must be motivated to succeed. If necessary, give a detailed briefing on the task in hand, so that there is no doubt in the delegatee's mind about what is expected from him. This will stir the subordinate to rise to the challenge and motivate him to succeed in the process. If the commander adopts an approach where he 'seemingly' consults the subordinate as regards the likely approach to the task in hand, the subordinate knows that the onus for smooth functioning has shifted to him. This method also allows the commander a chance to satisfy himself with regard to the professional competence of the delegatee, because his responses will indicate his interest, or lack of it where the particular responsibility is concerned. A lack of interest on the part of the subordinate does not mean that he has to be abandoned as a 'gone case'. If that happens, then the commander would be failing in his duty of training his command. All that it means is, that a commander may have to find a different method of motivating that subordinate. Maybe setting him up in competition with a peer would galvanise him into action, or conveying a sense of urgency and reiterated faith in his ability will help him overcome his reservations and the mental blocks that deter him from taking on responsibility. What a commander needs is not a set of rules or techniques, but good skills, both in diagnosing situations and in acting appropriately within them. Having delegated a task, one pitfall to be avoided is to keep asking, "How is it going?"[13] ("Controlling, stifling people, keeping them in the dark, wasting their time on trivia and reports. Breathing down their necks. You cannot manage self-confidence into people." Jack Welch) In all likelihood the subordinate may interpret it as cogent evidence of the higher commander's lack of faith in his ability to complete the task without such a show of concern and intervention. Therefore, it might be more appropriate to describe benchmarks to indicate the progress of work if it is a 'time bound' programme. The subordinate can be informed of the 'landmarks' he has to reach in a particular timeframe. The sole object of the exercise must be to provide the subordinate with an open-ended opportunity to recount progress, rather than what could become an easy escape route for either functionary. A continual "running audit" of the subordinate's skills and experience is of primary importance to a leader who wishes to succeed. This "running audit" should also provide the subordinate with an opportunity to chip in with suggestions and opinions where fast and economical completion of the assignment is concerned. A commander will do well to listen to these, because it is more likely that a man actually carrying out a task will discover appropriate short cuts and simpler ways of doing things. (*"We are constantly amazed by how much people will do when they are* not *told what to do by the superiors. The reason is that much of the creativity and innovation that enhances productivity lay with those who are closest to the actual work. Clearly, those who actually do the work have some striking ideas on how things could be done better."* —Jack Welch.)

- **Whose duty is it to maintain a high level of professional competence where his subordinates are concerned?** Reposing more confidence in a junior officer is likely to pay better dividends in the long run. (A man who is given freedom to fail will succeed more often than he fails.) A particular piece of the management lingo, which is a favourite with commanders who do not wish to take risks with their subordinates, is "organisational climate". They are firmly of the opinion that the present generation of juniors does not have their kind of *'josh'* and commitment to the cause. They are convinced that the climate is therefore not suitable for giving their subordinates a free hand to make mistakes and learn from them. To those who say that it is difficult to bring back the ethics and commitment of the earlier days a story of a famous French Marshal will be relevant. Marshal Lyautey once asked his gardener to plant a certain type of tree. The gardener protested that the tree was slow growing and would not reach maturity for a hundred years. The Marshal replied, "In that case, there is no time to lose; plant it this afternoon". We cannot accept a slide in professionalism just because it will be too tedious and time consuming to put the show back on the road. Some painful decisions will have to be taken in order to ensure that the focus of the juniors remains on professionalism and practicality. Of course, there will be a need for some changes and differences in the approach of the higher commander while he is at it. Maybe, there will be an element of risk involved where a commander is concerned. Unfortunately, the system also does not permit a commander to take any risks, because the subordinate's performance has a direct bearing on the commander's own professional profile. In the process what is forgotten is the fact that 'delegation' is the means by which a commander's most valuable asset, his subordinates, are exercised and developed to the sensible limits of individual capability and potential.

Create involvement-Set up Quality Circles

"QC is many things-meetings, team-building, training. But its central objective is "growing" a culture where everyone's ideas have value, everyone plays a part, where leaders lead rather than control".

—Jack Welch, CEO of General Electric.

We all agree that in today's world behavioural aspects assume additional importance when an effort is made to knit any team, create total involvement and achieve quality. The degree of individual commitment to the usually mundane (perceived) task bears a reasonably constant relation to the degree of deep satisfaction one experiences when the task becomes almost second nature. If the task relates to efficient and effective soldiering it assumes an added importance, because there could be situations when a soldierly skill could save lives or lead to gaining a tactical advantage. During their peace tenure, units are expected to rest, recoup and train. The process also involves bringing their equipment back to normal and readying themselves for their next sojourn to the operational areas. This is the time to bring in cohesiveness in the sections and platoons.

In the USA, elements of the Defence Department have been exploring the utilisation of Quality Circles as leadership and management tools. It has been felt that a Quality Circle's understanding about the methods and means of doing things is an exceedingly powerful force in determining the creative potential of the members. To achieve a high level of performance you can set up Quality Circles (QCs) in your units. A QC is a sub group formed by people from a work group, whose task is to develop ways to better accomplish their task. It often means trying out new ideas. Many ideas grow better when transplanted into another mind. A QC is a constructive medium for generating and developing 'creative intelligence'. Thus, QC primarily means a common effort for improving the performance of a unit or sub unit. Common effort is the result of common intentions. Common intentions require commonly accepted and acceptable aims. These, in turn are the outcome of shared needs. The needs could relate to improving speed in loading a weapon system, or restoring a weapon to its serviceability when it has a minor problem that could have come about because of a faulty loading or firing drill. QC is basically a small group of people, involved in similar work, who volunteer to meet periodically to discuss quality problems, investigate causes, recommend solutions and take corrective actions to the extent of their authority. These modular or task-group structures are, of necessity, based on the principle of teamwork and problem solving. The fundamental purposes of QCs are:

(a) **To Contribute to the improvement and development of the enterprise**. Human behaviour is goal oriented. The attitude of individuals towards their unit, its performance and their own contribution is a major factor in providing synergy, harmony and growth. Motivational and other behavioural techniques are used to bring about the necessary attitudinal changes. The Japanese have made major strides in this field. They could be called pioneers in 'team building' through 'quality circle movement'. Circle activities should be so designed that morale is gradually elevated, or rather morale becomes elevated as a natural consequence of taking part in the activity. Harmonious relations should bloom spontaneously as flowers do. Recognition of the good work done by a circle and appreciation at an appropriate level can be a big morale-boosting factor.

(b) **Respect humanity and build a happy, bright working environment that is meaningful to the people.** When an individual joins up as an officer or as another rank he hardly has any specific knowledge or training for undertaking assignments that are likely to come his way while he grows in service. It is for the superior officers to identify those traits and qualities that make an individual incline towards a particular skill, and thus make him an important member of the team. There are any number of junior officers and other ranks who are clearly ahead of their contemporaries in a diverse range of military skills. If a commander does not have his finger on the pulse of his command, he may not be able to identify these potential leaders. The subordinate may feel neglected and ignored in the absence of this recognition and chance to display his capabilities. Soon enough he may lose interest in the job and become only a mechanical performer so as to keep himself out of trouble or being branded a "shammer". If such a situation arises, the onus is on the immediate superior and the commander who have allowed a talent to be subdued or to wither away because they had no time or inclination to motivate a subordinate to be trained, groomed and be ready for higher assignment. One of the prime advantages of Quality Circle is that the process induces a healthy and much needed sense of importance in subordinates. Such a feeling leads to that golden asset; pride in one's work-the first step towards higher levels of efficiency. A soldier has his own aspirations, worries, needs and values. Merging these into the organisational goals can easily be achieved in 'quality circles' because a QC allows commanders to identify those individual needs in an atmosphere where free and frank discussions form the basis of every activity. Identification of common goals and encouraging creativity helps in bonding people together.

(c) **Display human capabilities fully and eventually draw out infinite possibilities.** This will give an opportunity to the members to use their ingenuity, experience and various skills. Originality and not conventionality should be the theme running through the entire exercise.[14] All the members should be encouraged to project their imagination and knowledge. An ideal thing to do would be to seek the views of those who could just be shy or lacking in confidence. Such a small group is the right platform to draw them out. It is possible that some of them could come up with solutions to any real or perceived problems facing the community.[15] In this, involvement of the officers should be minimal. Ideally, after introducing the concept and putting the show on the road, no senior officer should monitor the proceedings. Even junior officers should be withdrawn once the JCOs and NCOs have understood the concept. The junior leaders should be encouraged to form QCs where the small groups could interact and device new and more effective and efficient ways of using resources. If some soldiers are also included in the 'think tanks', it ensures better involvement and participation. A routine training event at platoon or company level should become a place where people can think and use their wisdom so as to improve the team's performance. Suggestions emerging from the QC meetings should be carefully examined and where possible, technically and tactically implemented. Feedback must be given to the 'circle'. This will help in meeting the objective of allowing every soldier to become a thinker, a planner and one who is sure that he is contributing towards the organisational goal. To be more effective, the commander must get around and show interest in what his subordinates are doing even if he does not know much about the technique of their work. A commander wanting to know more about the task in hand will generate tremendous enthusiasm, but he should facilitate rather than control, so that subordinates develop confidence in themselves and their equipment. (*I do not propose to lay down for you a plan of campaign; but simply to lay down the work it is desirable to have done and leave you free to execute it in your own way.*

—General Ulysses S Grant)

It is worth remembering that it is relatively easy to command regular soldiers in peacetime. They are volunteers for the job and can be trained and tuned according to the organisational needs. Officers only have to be good enough to command all types of soldiers, whatever walk of life they come from, or whatever their calibre may be. QCs provide one forum where the all round development of a soldier and organisational well being can be given an appropriate shape. A contemporary and hi-tech Army needs to develop a more team-oriented culture in order to maximise the efforts and initiatives of small groups of people. A 'group' solution in handling and manning complicated weapon systems found via a QC will do tons of good and lift morale of troops. While technology provides a base for superior performance, it is inevitably up to the human resources to use that technology to its highest potential, in order to help the organisation reach its most far-reaching and challenging goals and objectives. A QC is an ideal forum for putting to good use the creative, constructive and imaginative capacities of the subordinates. The approach is appealing because it combines the solid elements of other human relations' approaches with skill training that will allow group members to become leaders in task performance. It motivates them to master those skills that are necessary for attaining the highest level of professional competence. The leadership has to be 'top class' for achieving best results. Without a high level of motivation and top class leadership, the technological capabilities are likely to remain under-utilised and less-than-optimally applied.

Sanctity of Chain of Command

There is a feeling rampant that the 'chain of command' unnecessarily delays action when urgency is called for. A sad pitfall today is the tendency to give orders to someone who is two or three levels below a commander. Not only are these commanders afraid of their own mistakes, they are unwilling to permit their juniors to learn by the best means available — experience through trial and error. Such commanders do not realise that these junior leaders in the chain of command are commanders in their own right and they are responsible for what their sub unit does or fails to do. Often enough one sees senior commanders, in their effort to ensure speed in action, take recourse to shortcuts and reach down. The by-passed junior leader may not even be aware of the assignment to his command. This kind of approach puts both the leader and the lead in a rather awkward position. The men may be flattered to work directly for the top level and may even be more responsive and enthusiastic, particularly if they are not overtly impressed by the professional competence of the junior leader. This is a dangerous trap and commanders sometimes do fall into it when they are in a hurry to show results, either to a visiting politician or even to an organisational dignitary. The laurels of success may thus be ensured for the commander, whereas a failure, in all likelihood, will be wrongly attributed to the junior leader. And unfortunately, failure in such a situation, when the men are under pressure to show results, is more likely than success. The harm thus caused to the 'by-passed' junior leader can do incalculable damage to the organisation as well as the morale of that junior. Naturally, mutual distrust is likely to creep in.

I know of a very senior officer who, while working in the Army Headquarters, invariably went to the functional levels in the first instance itself, on the premise that the babus generally know every case by heart because they have been there for much longer than the officers. Initially, the clerical staff (a mix of military and civil) responded with zeal and enthusiasm while his officers sulked for having been left out of the action. But the enthusiasm levels of the staff declined in due course of time because they could not sustain the hectic pace of responding to all kinds of queries raised by their boss while answering those from the ministry of defence. Functional level officers who had been unhappy were suddenly finding a lot to laugh about behind their harried superior's back. This was a typical "service" headquarters atmosphere where the babus liked to work at their own pace with their frequent 'tea-breaks', and they had no reason to continue humouring the boss. Luckily for all concerned, the senior officer 'cooled down' after sensing the mood and measuring motivation levels of his staff, and perhaps, with some friendly advice from his peers who had experienced the "work culture" of the headquarters. In service headquarters this kind of attitude can perhaps be absorbed because no real damage is done to the institution. The problem arises in formations and units committed operationally, where it is not uncommon for some of the brigade commanders to reach down to the company or even platoon levels without taking the commanding officer in confidence. This method of ensuring speed in action, inter alia, leads to letting down your subordinate and could have an adverse effect on the morale of the junior commanders. (Reducing "layers" for functional efficiency is sometimes confused with bypassing the chain. Commanders need to guard against this tendency. And if, for some reason, it is operationally essential to reach down, then the immediate commander of the sub unit must be informed, so that he could either confirm the lower level's input and/or add to it.)

In war there may be situations where the failure of a junior leader could lead to disaster and it may be imperative for a more experienced superior to take charge of the situation. But it should be an exception; even then the by-passed junior leader if taken into confidence could contribute some important bit of intimate knowledge of the terrain or the opposition. His motivation to be useful towards the organisational goal will thus be ensured. The men will also look up to their platoon and company commanders when they know that the officer has been accepted as a competent leader of men even when the chips are down. The tendency of senior civil officials and ministers to rush to every site of a mishap is a clear indication of distrust in their subordinates and their training. This is hardly likely to induce the junior leader on the spot to display any initiative because he knows that sooner rather than later some superior will come and start undoing all that he had done to bring back normalcy. This does not mean that a higher commander should keep himself aloof from the day-to-day life of the troops under his command. Instead, a commander will contribute tremendously if he is receptive to initiations from below, even conceding on some issues just to aid junior leaders to maintain and build their standing with the troops they lead and communicate through these junior leaders only. This gives the junior confidence that he has a superior who is there to protect him from errors that could be due to lack of experience and exposure. One 'grows' under the benign guidance of such a leader. The overall personality of the superior, to live up to these requirements, must entail professional competence, an ear to the ground and an ability to economise on effort. His ability to think, plan ahead, examine present limitations and capabilities of the subordinate commanders, and then assign tasks will give him a better chance of success instead of continuously and consistently asking for feedback, reports and such like.

Leadership must be distributed. Your subordinate commanders cannot move forward effectively in the absence of that big picture. They cannot self-test and self-review without adequate feedback, cannot count on each other without trust in common and widespread moral wisdom. Distributed leadership integrates the paradoxes inherent in human association. We need to recover the old-fashioned wisdom that one of the primary jobs of leadership is to develop ethical and practical awareness in people, while bringing out their creativity and professional competence. It does require each of us to begin cultivating our ethical competence with the same enthusiasm and dedication that we devote to cultivating our technical and other soldierly skills. There is a requirement to cultivate these qualities and superimpose them on the basic personality of an individual leader of troops. In essence, a higher commander is expected to assess trainability of his subordinates and groom them for higher responsibility.

Management by Walking Around

Leadership must be active, not passive; authority must be exercised to be accepted by those who are to carry out orders. "One look", said George Patton, "is better than two reports." Anticipating trouble requires very close contact with what is happening on the ground. A commander can listen to any number of briefings, but if he does not go to the scene of action, he has no clear-cut idea of what it is all about. A constant touch with the subordinates allows a leader to understand the thinking and the planned next moves of the key members of his team. It has become all the more relevant and important now for the commanders to be seen by their men fairly regularly because of the isolation and other problems that men deployed on CI duties suffer from. This helps a commander to make personal contact with as many people as possible. Often enough, commanders tend to put off such interaction for a number of reasons. Principal among them is inadequacy of time and the heap of paperwork and the conferences in distant headquarters that consume most of their energy. But to be true to his vocation, a commander has to find time and energy for this task. I can recommend the approach of a battalion commander whom I had seen in action in J&K. An extremely effective method adopted by this battalion commander, while deployed in the operational area, was creative, constructive and result oriented. He had developed a sort of "crude" golf course connecting most of the pickets and posts occupied by his troops. Almost everyday after having finished with the paper and other work at the battalion headquarters he would "tee-off" usually accompanied by his Regimental Medical Officer (RMO). The two would halt at the pickets and while the RMO went through the 'sick parade' at the post, the CO would have an informal talk with the troops. Over a hot cup of tea, the men, in addition to the official and operational situation as it pertained to their area of responsibility, tended to share their personal worries and domestic problems with the CO, who was otherwise too far removed from a lowly soldier and his problems. Incidentally, the most common complaint of the soldier is his frustration at being unable to express himself to anyone having more authority than his immediate superior, without bearing the stigma of having by-passed the proper channels. In the instant case no such situation arose because the immediate superior was not by-passed in any manner and the soldier was being given a chance to informally interact with his commanding officer. Where possible, immediate action was taken to rectify the situation or advice rendered. Not every problem of the troops was solved. But the fact that the issue had been taken up with the "father" of the unit helped an individual's spirit and generated tremendous goodwill and faith in the commanding officer, and the CO did not have to find "time" to visit posts held by his troops. This CO was very clear in his mind that sensitivity to others and empathy would help in gaining the confidence of the subordinates. The twosome (CO and the RMO, sometimes a new arrival to the unit was also taken along for an informal orientation of the area of responsibility) would take their lunch at any picket where they happened to be at 'mealtime'. This arrangement served the purpose of building up and sustaining the morale of troops. As it could never be predicted where the CO would be halting for lunch, the quality of food provided to the troops was the best in the entire formation. The time and effort saved by the troops in coming to the "Regimental Aid Post" even for minor ailments was curtailed. Also the CO was not required to go through lengthy 'situational reports' every-day? Suiting an individual style and job content, many such innovations can be made so as to have a finger on the pulse. The thing to remember is that warmth facilitates the establishment of rapport with the subordinates. A display of warmth is particularly effective when one is new to an assignment and the subordinates do not know one well enough. Any leader who desires unvarnished feedback about his command must establish channels of his own that supplement his chain of command. This does not mean that the prescribed channels of communications be eliminated or compromised. The fact of the matter is, that the chain of command is irrefutably the quickest and most dependable method for a commander to disseminate information to his troops. But it does not provide sufficiently reliable means to keep a commander informed of the feelings and attitudes of his men with regards to this information. It is therefore important that a commanding officer has an informal means of interaction with his men.

One question that frequently arises is, "How can I delegate and decentralise and still know what is going on?" That is where 'management by walking around comes in'. Delegation of responsibility actually frees the commander to have greater contact with his troops and thus increase his knowledge of what is happening. The more functions he retains for his own performance, the more he is tied to his desk and to day-to-day responsibilities and the less opportunities he has to know his troops and their activities. One should appear 'casual' and relaxed, keeping one's eyes and ears open, evaluating the proceedings and planning for corrective action while walking around. This helps one perform better and enhances all round efficiency.

A clear line of authority where no one has to report to more than one superior helps in defining responsibility and authority clearly. Responsibility is meaningless if it is not coupled with authority. The responsibility of the higher authority for the act of the subordinates is absolute even if a task or an assignment has been delegated. Authority should be delegated as far down the line as possible, and the number of levels of authority should be kept to the minimum. The assignment of every member of the team should normally be confined, as far as possible, to the performance of a single leading function. In the case of Ordnance depots and EME workshops, whenever possible, line functions should be separated from staff functions (it is not unusual for a sub depot commander to be doubling up as the quartermaster in our depots). In this era of "officer's shortage" too many assignments are being given to young officers without realising that there is a limit to the number of positions that can be co-ordinated or controlled by a single individual. For better results it would be more appropriate if the organisation were kept flexible. And it should be kept as simple as possible. Successful commanders operate effectively because of knowledge of organisational requirements, and of how the human elements in their charge may be combined, balanced, and directed toward ultimate objectives.

Leadership qualities are not God given gifts. There are very few leadership qualities that could be termed as God given. Most others can be developed by conscious effort. Montgomery says in his memoirs, "many men who are not natural leaders may have some small spark of the qualities which are needed. This spark must be looked for and then developed and brought out by training." Seniors can help their juniors develop qualities like initiative, judgement, decisiveness, and physical courage by training and providing appropriate guidance. It has been said that there are three kinds of people in the world-those who make things happen, those who watch things happen and those who don't know what is happening. Leaders are supposed to fall in the first of these categories because their specific purpose is to make things happen. It is necessary therefore, that a leader knows: what has to happen, what action is required to make it happen, how it should happen and how it is happening. But it is not as simple as that. No individual, whatever his inherent intellectual ability and qualities of character and leadership, could perform these functions efficiently without considerable training and experience.

Chapter 5

Communication Skills

"Someone somewhere has a better idea. Communicate, and then communicate again".—Jack Welch, CEO.

"A key element in determining a manager's potential for advancement is his skill in communication".

—Rawleigh Warner, Jr Chairman Mobil Corporation, USA

How often does it happen that when you shout at a subordinate for not having carried out the designated task in the manner you had prescribed his first reaction is that of surprise. This surprise is then generally followed by a resigned look, drooping of shoulders or even a muttered curse under his breath for having wasted all that effort and energy in doing what he thought was his actual assignment. The real trouble was that he had not clearly understood the requirement. For want of efficient and effective communication neither had he followed your original briefing, nor had you cared to ensure that your instructions to him had been fully comprehended. The ability to communicate and listen effectively is perhaps the most important skill at a leader's command—all other professional skills depend on it. In any appreciation of leadership skills, good communication between various levels of functioning has been identified as an essential requirement. Almost three-fourths of an individual's working hours are spent in talking, listening or writing to others. At the beginning of a career a young officer earns respect of his subordinates and appreciation of his superiors by his conduct, professional competence and willingness to learn. The higher you go, the wider is the spread of communication because then one is interacting at different levels. Communication extends not only to more people below but also to different levels above, it extends sideways and to other departments and wings. This is where effort put in to develop appropriate communication skills at the beginning of the career starts paying off. Listening patiently to your subordinates makes them feel that what they are saying is important towards achieving the organisational goal. A leader who learns to listen and encourages his subordinates to listen and ask questions gives them a sense of participation. Two-way communication, in fact, is the most effective leadership tool, be it industry or the military. Like anything else, the ability to communicate clearly, effectively and persuasively is a skill that can be learnt. Careful listening, clear, concise and precise writing are important ingredients of effective communication.

> *When I ask you to listen to me, and you start giving advice, you have not done what I asked. When I ask you to listen to me and you begin to tell me why I shouldn't feel that way, you are trampling on my feelings.*
>
> *When I ask you to listen to me you feel you have to do something to solve my problems, you have failed me, strange, as that may seem.*
>
> *Listen! All I ask is that you listen, not to talk or do—just hear me.*
>
> *When you do something for me that I can and need to do for myself, you contribute to my fear and inadequacy.*
>
> *And I can do for myself; I am not helpless. May be discouraged and faltering, but not helpless.*

But when you accept as a simple fact that I do feel what I feel, no matter how irrational, then I quit trying to convince you and get about the business of understanding what's behind this irrational feeling. And when that's clear, the answers are obvious and I don't need advice.

God just listens and lets you work it out for yourself.

So please listen and just hear me. And if you want to talk, wait a minute for your turn and I will listen to you.

—Ralph Roughton

Learn to Listen

Listening is a critical facet of communication. The leaders of the American industry quoted above found the right formula for success. In their perception it was their listening skill and ability to communicate that was one of the main ingredients in their success in building up the empires that they did. Getting people to talk frankly, openly and at some length requires an ability to listen, to be silent for long enough periods to draw out the other person. This is particularly important when our other ranks have not yet got over the inhibition that generally prevents them from talking to an officer as a professional colleague. To break this psychological barrier an officer will be required to have the ability to synchronise his own speech pattern to the pattern of others, so that subordinates develop enough confidence and faith in the leader and his communication skills. This becomes more difficult when soldiers are required to interact with a higher commander and are not very sure about the reaction and response to their observations. A very long time back when the Indian Army was equipped with Chevrolet and Ford vehicles, the situation got to be particularly bad-where vehicle availability was concerned-in a formation. The commander himself went to the workshop where the JCO was in charge (the officer commanding that particular workshop was on leave). The formation commander found that most of the Chevrolet vehicles were 'off road' for want of gearboxes, and some other major assemblies; and in the case of Ford vehicles, engines were required. To improve the vehicle availability he directed that "cannibalisation" should be undertaken and Chevrolet engines be fitted on the other make. The JCO tried to explain that it was not possible to do so because of technical problems. The commander thought this to be the usual bellyache of a support service; and the JCO, in order to avoid further displeasure, gave up trying to make him understand the reasons why the commander's orders could not be carried out. The morale of the workshop staff remained low till the OC workshop returned, and learnt about the commander's visit during his absence and the impact of unworkable orders on his men. He immediately went to the formation commander to inform him that his orders were technically impossible. He told him that whereas a Chevrolet was a "six cylinder" engine the Ford had eight cylinders. There was no commonality between the two vehicles other than the fact that these both were 'load carriers'. The commander had to withdraw his order and as word got around about this gaffe, considerable embarrassment was caused to him. If only he had listened to that JCO, who in any case had never been talked to by such a high ranking officer and was naturally under a lot of nervous pressure while answering questions, all this need not have happened.

One thing becomes clear from the above episode. Open communication does much to help commanders become aware of the realities of situations and it gives them more complete inputs for decision-making. Another thing is, senior officers have a tendency to underestimate the natural intelligence of the subordinates, particularly if the subordinates happen to be from 'other ranks'. If a subordinate is not allowed to communicate with the commander in a manner that allows him a frank expression of his assessment of a problem or a situation, the higher commander may not get a true and real picture. A senior may find himself in a position where straightforward information gets denied to him, either by design or by default. It will do no harm if a commander lets it be known and passed around that he is always open to communication from his subordinates, who can and should convey to him any information even if it is not positive and might be connected to failure. A deep abiding belief in yourself is essential if you are to hear people out when they are saying something you may not want to hear.

Become a creative and constructive listener. Your open-minded approach is crucial in instilling confidence in your subordinates that they can share their 'professional' opinions and views with you without any fear. In the first chapter of Bhagwad Gita, Arjuna decided not to fight. Sri Krishna did not interrupt him when he was giving his reasons for this thought process. He gave him a patient hearing. He noted Arjuna's feelings and thoughts but did not interfere and kept silent. While responding to Arjuna's sentiments (Bhagwad Gita chapter 2) Sri Krishna dealt with the issues involved in a manner that would motivate Arjuna. The process included five stages:

- Listening patiently.
- Putting stress on positive aspects and strengths of own side.
- Discussing the issues involved on an intellectual level.
- Defining the action plan to achieve the desired goals.
- Highlighting the consequences/results of the proposed action plan.

A subordinate can grow only when he is given opportunity to express his ideas and to contribute his suggestions before his superior takes action on matters which involve him. In this way the, the leader creates an inclusive, challenging and nurturing environment that enables others to develop their fullest potential. Through participation of this kind the subordinate becomes more and more aware of his superior's problems and worries. Resultantly, he gets genuine satisfaction in knowing that his ideas and opinions are given consideration in the search for solutions.

" If there is anyone secret of success, it lies in the ability to get the other person's point of view and see things from his angle as well as your own." —Henry Ford

When complete inputs are not available to the commander, or when the subordinates think that all angles have not been examined, their response to orders from the higher commander cannot be enthusiastic. There are those who contend that the best strategist is the commander most distantly removed from his troops. No commander can become a strategist until he knows his men. The strong, distant, placid and silent types, idealised and idolised in fiction and cinema are not the leaders of the real world. No amount of personnel work can make people think you care about them if they never see you, or never get a chance to interact with you on a 'person to person' level. Accessibility of the commander is indispensable to effective communication. And it must be coupled with developing the confidence among subordinates that they will not be penalised for reporting bad news or for their openness and candour. For a conversation to be frank and honest there should be very little contradiction and interference from the commander. But officers sometimes tend to be too concerned about what they want to communicate next, instead of listening for sometimes buried ideas and beliefs that the men under command are trying to communicate. Very often our conversations become monologues and we do not understand what really is going on inside another human being. The commander only has to listen to his men for them to contribute wholeheartedly towards the successful completion of a mission. Similarly, a commander who cannot communicate, or worse, who does not want to communicate, can put no principles or guidelines on efficient and effective leadership into action below a particular level of his command.

"I hadn't yet learned what I know now- that the ability to communicate is everything."
—Lee Iacocca, Chairman and CEO Chrysler Corporation

It is an accepted fact that higher commanders can rely on the indirect influencing process only in proportion to their level in hierarchy. In any case it is difficult for a higher commander to communicate with troops on a regular basis, busy as he is. But can a subordinate have access to him? Many commanders with considerable responsibilities do not know even the names of officers working in their headquarters. A large number of them never see, or are seen by their senior staff officers who belong to the "support services". I know of a famous corps commander who saw his Service Heads (other than the medical representative, of course) only on their arrival in his formation or when they got posted out. As far as he was concerned they were only "decoration pieces" while attending his conferences. They were neither expected to have any opinion on matters military, nor were they expected to express any. (Even where the subject concerned them or was relevant in the realm of material support, they were to put up opinions through his "general staff" channel.) These commanders tend to overlook the obvious. Jack Welch says, "Layers insulate. They slow things down. They garble things. Leaders in highly layered organisations are like people who wear several sweaters on a freezing winter day. They remain warm and comfortable but are blissfully ignorant of the realities of their environment. They couldn't be further from what is going on." Any reluctance to talk to subordinates always creates a barrier. If the leader is accessible even when he is otherwise busy, the subordinate naturally respects him.

An active listener grasps both facts and feelings, and that is what endears him to his subordinates. Maybe, that is why God gave us two ears and only one tongue, which gently hints that we should listen more and talk less. Listening requires two ears, one for meaning and one for feeling. Most communication becomes ineffective because most of us are poor listeners. The reason for poor listening is that a normal person speaks at the rate of approximately 150 words per minute, while we have the capacity to listen to over 1,000 words per minute. The difference makes for a wandering mind. A major problem is the fact that most commanders really do not expect substantial and meaningful two-way communication. Real listening is a skill that most leaders need to develop. All that one requires is the ability to listen effectively, to be silent for long enough periods to draw out the men one commands.

A central point about communication on the part of an effective leader or manager is simply that it is going on all the time, and is a two-way process. Verbal communications can be effective only if these are on a face-to-face basis and are interactive. Where the communication is from a different location, there could be some problem in identifying with the communicator. However, if the communicator is a well-known personality and his voice is easily recognisable over the medium, and the men are tuned into him, then the task of a leader becomes somewhat easier. Modern communication methods (particularly television) have made it easier for a leader to project an image of himself and his approach to the mission in hand, to a vast number of troops concurrently.

Watch your own communication

"Once a word goes out of your mouth, you can never swallow it again."

—A Russian Proverb

More often than not, commanders get going with their pontificating without judging the reactions of their audience. They are in a great hurry to get the material off their chests, without realising that subordinates also judge their leaders; and they judge, not the length of the speech, but its quality and content. There is no point in conveying one sentence in two paragraphs. Therefore, clarify your own ideas, consult with others where appropriate, and make room for their opinions in planning your communication. Examine the true purpose in each case beforehand. Consider the total physical and human setting and convey something of help or value to the receiver. In the case of verbal communication, be mindful of the overtones as well as the basic contents of your message. A leader has to watch for any "communication overload" developing. Such a situation can very easily sidetrack the main issue, creating confusion and wasteful effort. Leaders must have a clear view of what is needed and what is feasible.

Today the personal touch—being concerned with a man's problem and being involved in all activities—is important because rank does not actually scare too many of our soldiers. It is even more important for a junior leader to be seen as a 'caring commander' who is concerned with the comforts and needs of the men under his command. The unit is the soldier's home and family because his own near and dear ones are far-removed. In such circumstances letters from home play a vital role in sustaining his morale. If these letters bring problems and the soldier has someone with whom he can discuss these, someone who can give practical help and advice, he is content. It must be remembered that normal training events and functioning are too involved and intricate these days for either the men or the officers to take serious note of personalities. One must create informal avenues for exchange of information, for getting a feel of the unit's pulse. For a junior commander it is relatively easy to find an appropriate time and place for creating an environment where his subordinates can unburden themselves in an informal manner. He can create such opportunities on the playing field, or during 'breaks' in a training session. During return to the lines after a long route march or a patrolling exercise is a good time to get your men to open up. Very often this does not happen. Perhaps these leaders are afraid of being thought paternalistic and out of tune with the modern age.

Insofar as a commanding officer is concerned, he can have an 'open house' once a week when anybody can walk in, discuss whatever problem, real or imaginary, he is facing. More often than not, with better perception and education, a commander can render help or advice in the men's domestic affairs as well, or write a note to local or civil authorities. He may not be able to resolve the issue, but having genuinely tried to do so, he will make his men more responsive to his command. It is absolutely essential to generate this faith by being seen as helpful to the men. Only then will the men think of their collective well-being as an issue of concern for the commanding officer and thus come forward with their useful and constructive suggestions. Field Marshal Slim says, "One need not be an orator to be effective. Two things only were necessary, first to know what you were talking about, and, second and most important, to believe it yourself. I found that if one kept the bulk of one's talk to the material things the men were interested in, food, pay, leave, mail and the progress of operations, it was safe to end on a higher note-the spiritual foundations-and I always did".

Learn to Read Body Language

Many leaders believe that they have done everything the moment they have issued orders, and they order a great deal because they find too many things out of tune with their thinking. In reality there are very few orders and instructions which receive immediate and unanimous approval of the subordinates. Notwithstanding the fact that the Army trains its people to obey and follow orders without any reluctance, it cannot prevent them from thinking. Soldiers are seldom passive observers of the events that occur around them. They form impressions about their leaders and the events that affect them. They respond to a particular situation based on their positive or negative evaluation. Very often a commander is required to convey ideas and information to the troops under his command. Sometimes what is being communicated is not what the subordinates have been hoping for, or expecting. In such situations, remember to 'take the temperature'. A leader should learn to study the expressions on the faces of those around him and notice what they are doing. They could be sitting back with their arms folded in an expression of withdrawal or leaning forward, tensed up with something they would perhaps like to say or are hoping to hear; they may be nodding with approval or frowning with anxiety. If feelings seem to be moving towards acceptance then, of course, a commander can get on with his exhortations for putting the 'best foot forward' and all that. However, if you feel that the atmosphere is going against what you want done, then unless it is an operationally urgent task, a commander could very well taper off. He could end the session suggesting that the proposal or the proposed action is at a "thinking stage" and would need a few more inputs before a decision gets taken. Theatricals won't work with today's jawan. In their hurry to be accepted as "one of the boys" some commanders tend to play to the gallery. They neither have the elan of a 'Patton' nor the qualities of a "Sam" to carry it off. Our soldier is intelligent enough to see through any charade of false comradeship and he will in all probability, associate this with lack of professional competence in the leader. All that is required is an ability to be forthright, knowledgeable, professionally sound and apparently honest. It is better to be natural and normal, which actually means neither concealing nor making a display of theatricals, and will pay better dividends in the form of loyalty and commitment from your subordinates. However, it is an established fact that a military leader, with an extrovert trait often generates more confidence in his subordinates, particularly when things are not going as per plans. The leader's presence should be used only when it can be seen as a requisite for moving men to actions that are essential to accomplishing the mission. That is, don't do it unless you are sure that you are the one who is needed on the spot to do the job. Inspiration and impulse are not synonymous where leadership is concerned. The impact that a leader has on the subordinate's psyche, the way he inspires confidence and conducts himself in trying situations is what leadership boils down to. He creates an environment where people motivate themselves to deliver.

A leader must know what causes a particular pattern of behaviour in his subordinates. It is important for him to do so, because only then can he identify the emotions that trigger a particular reaction in an individual. It is all the more important for a commander who has just taken over the command and is familiarising himself with the operational situation, to show a human face. It will help people recognise him as a normal human being who can be reached and therefore, can be trusted with one's life. A commander must test the reactions of his men and must sense when there is likely to be a feeling of resentment. This does not mean that you have to put the subject to vote or any thing like that. A clear and frank picture of the situation, asking for suggestions from the more senior of your subordinates, could ease the tension when the assigned task is going to be uncomfortable, dangerous or difficult. There is an urgent need for adjusting one's behaviour to the responses of one's subordinates.

Do not be secretive

Earlier we have discussed the 'principle of taking your men into confidence'. So how is this one any different from that? It is. Look at it this way, you pass an order to your men to be ready for an immediate move to another post, when they have just finished with their digging and laying defences at the present one. They are tired and have been looking forward to a bit of rest after a hard day's work. Instead, they have been put to further activity that was not made clear when the task was originally assigned. To a soldier this means that his commander had held something back when directions and orders for the task were initially given to him. This means, even the next move may not be the last and the men will be put to inconvenience again and again, without any tangible gain or improvement in the operational situation. A marathon runner undergoes all the hardships of a gruelling race because he knows that his activity will end at a particular spot and the task will finish. Now imagine the same runner being unsure of the direction, distance and the likely duration of his race. Where is the motivation for him to put in that bit of extra effort to end his task in a manner that gives him satisfaction? Similar is the case with men. If an assignment is not explained in the first instance, you can rest assured that through the 'grapevine' or "langar gup" the men will broadly know what is coming up. The 'grapevine' is especially fast and active when the news is significant and is likely to have a direct impact on the rank and file. Unless the formal communication system is fast, reliable and flexible, the 'grapevine' is likely to dominate the flow of information down the ladder. In the absence of comprehensible information giving-the whys and wherefores of asking men to perform a task that they feel they can do without-rumours gain credence. And since the 'grapevine' has no reliable source to which participants can refer, to confirm those inputs, it carries rumour or distorted information rather easily. (The unfortunate episode of revolt by the brave 'Sikh soldiers' in the wake of Operation Blue Star would perhaps have never taken place if the men had been taken into confidence in the first place. Rumours, fed and flamed by some disgruntled elements, caused problems that the Indian Army is still trying to live down.)

Today's soldier will not rest in ignorance because the wise sage said, "ignorance is bliss". He wants to know the whys and wherefores when he cannot comprehend the rationale behind some particular order or instruction. If uninstructed, he will be in a state of confused error. Therefore, it makes better sense to apprise him of the situation yourself. For whatever information is received by a soldier, whether in the form of rumour, gossip, speculation or official information, it will all be judged in terms of its supportive value to his psychological advantages. His perception of the environment will motivate his action and reaction. An obvious conclusion one can arrive at is-men must be taken into confidence at the earliest stage, before rumours gain credence in any way.

Written Communication

A commander, in order to get an enthusiastic response from his command must get across his personal skills, his intentions, encouragement and genuine concern for the system and the individuals who form the system. Towards this end, a good command on the written word and verbal skills is indispensable. Putting your thoughts and ideas in writing means greater assurance of their understanding and attainment. What's more important is the aspect that putting ideas in writing is a requisite of good communication. One finds that the reading and writing habit is virtually dying out. One can blame television and sundry other distractions, but the fact of the matter is that one finds young officers today who do not want to develop writing skills. They do not want to project any new thoughts and ideas. Among the many factors that work against an individual's expression of new thoughts are:

- Lack of time, real or imaginary. More often than not, it is imaginary. The work schedule for an officer, unless he is holding some high-pressure assignment, is not so tight that he cannot find half an hour a day to say something constructive on paper. There are any number of issues, both professional and personal, that have a direct impact on the day-to-day functioning of a unit or an individual. Any officer who keeps his eyes and ears open and can think rationally is capable of projecting his thoughts in a cogent manner on paper.

- The normal requirement of a thoroughly researched study as the vehicle for presentation of a new thought. This means a lot of reading is to be done before ideas are given shape. Not a particularly easy task if one is not inclined to read beyond 'filmy gossip'. Almost all formations and units have adequately equipped libraries. There is no real excuse for not using the facilities, except that there is not enough motivation to do so. Commanders should insist on their subordinates writing a "military paper" on a subject, at least once in three months. (Our ACR form has two columns where an officer is rated for his written and verbal skills. Commanders can make effective use of this endorsement, to encourage their subordinates. I had a system where officers were required to write papers on a wide range of subjects. Better efforts were even put up before 'inspecting officers' for their perusal.) A formalised system for the development of creative ideas will serve as an outlet and a stimulus for new thoughts. One never knows when someone will come up with something original or constructive that will help the organisation. Not all the participants will become 'intellectuals', but the exercise will make them think, and the act of writing will make them put these thoughts in a perspective that could actually trigger an overall improvement in a unit's functioning. It is difficult to capitalise on creative ideas unless one keeps a careful record of them. And there is no better way of doing so than by putting them on paper.

- The possibility that the proposed thoughts may differ from those of the individual's immediate superior. In an ACR driven army this is a real problem. Higher commanders can contribute a lot to the growth of youngsters, if they let the word go around that they actually enjoy a junior officer coming up with different and well-thought-out angles to various professional issues. And it is not as if all higher commanders dislike an opinion different from theirs. I have come across many senior officers who actually lock forward to somebody offering an opinion that differs from well-established norms or even their own views on military matters. Legend has it that George Patton had a placard displayed in his office which read, "A Staff Officer Who Does NOT Disagree Once In a While is Not Required in This Headquarter".
- Lack of confidence as typified by the feeling: "I am sure someone has already thought of this". So why should I waste time and effort in any research and writing. Another thing will be: "my article or paper may not be accepted for publication". George Bernard Shaw once said that the number of "regret notes" he received till he became famous could have 'wallpapered' his house. So what if nobody finds the write-up acceptable. The effort made would have taken you one step further towards better communication skills.

The basics of good communication skills can always be learnt. Broadly these are:

- A communication should convey a sense of character.
- It should not be a "civil service" type of monotone, where a leader reads through a prepared script without gauging the reactions of his audience.
- While being precise and terse, it should go beyond precision and brevity and need not be "telegraphic". But too much communication is as bad as too little. Tell people what they need to know; do not swamp them with information and exhortation.
- The content should be such that it is easily understood. Nobody is going to judge you by your command on the language; judgement will be based on the content. During air strikes by the Germans on London, Sir Winston Churchill addressed the nation saying, "I can offer you only blood, sweat and tears." These few words almost became a national chant during those trying days. With his command on the language and if he had only wanted to impress people he could as well have said, "The prospect whose imminence I have to communicate to you is characterised exclusively by features sanguinary, laborious and lachrymose." Not many people would have understood the Prime Minister's "message to the nation", and he couldn't have impressed his listeners either.
- Never be long winded. Do not try to express a sentence in two paragraphs. It follows that a leader who waxes eloquent and is long winded at the slightest opportunity, is usually throwing up a smokescreen to hide his own professional inadequacies. He could spend any amount of time in trying to explain what he wants done, he will not be able to communicate unless he is prepared well enough with his subject. Nothing puts off a recipient like a neatly bound, thick

folder that contains all garbage and hardly any constructive input.

- It should never be "they", but as far as possible, "we" and "us". Another thing to be guarded against is the use of negatives, more so when one is sending a written communication. For example, 'this is not to say that additional training would be unwarranted in all circumstances, nor that it could not be positively beneficial in certain cases.' The originator of this complex communication could have just as easily said 'additional training may be beneficial in certain cases.'

Check your Communication skills as per the following check list:

- How effectively do I listen, listening includes constructive responses that help other person express his thoughts and feelings.
- How many times do I interrupt a communication. Keep your emotions in the background
- How often do I contradict others
- Are conversations between me and subordinates frank and in confidence
- Do I keep misunderstandings to at a minimum or do I deliberately misunderstand
- Do I give the subordinates the impression that I want to hear the truth
- Do I give genuine ideas and thoughts or say things others want to hear
- How do I handle conflicting views
- How often are problems discussed with me
- Do I know the standards of performance for myself and my subordinates

- Do I know what it takes to do a task before I get others to do the same

Ten Commandments of Good Communication

- Clarify your ideas before communicating
- Examine the true purpose of each communication
- Consider the total physical and human setting whenever you communicate
- Consult others when appropriate in planning communication
- Be mindful, while you communicate, of overtones as well as the basic content of your message
- Take the opportunity, when it arises, to convey something of help or value to receiver
- Make sure you follow up your communication
- Communicate for tomorrow as well as for today
- Be sure your actions support your communication
- Seek not only to be understood but also to understand-endeavour to be good listener

Chapter 6

Role of Rites and Rituals

"Tradition does not mean that you never do anything new, but that you never fall below the standard of courage and conduct handed down to you. Then, tradition far from being handcuffs to cramp your action, will be handrails to guide and steady you in rough places"

—Field Marshal Slim

The army today is an institution in transition, profoundly affected by historical events, political processes, economic forces and social change, while sustaining a deep continuity of traditions and institutional practices. History is loaded with examples of what can be accomplished by groups of people who are motivated by enlightened self-interest and a desire to perform. Traditional wisdom or intuition that worked in the past may not work with the soldiers of today. For somebody to make the ultimate sacrifice of his life for a cause, he ought to have lived with certain ideologies and beliefs. These could be latent traits of the individual, or ingrained after joining the Army. Ideology is defined as an organisation of compatible beliefs, and it must be morally acceptable. Where 'belief' is concerned, it must be rooted in the tradition of the country; and the beliefs should be such that they are retained throughout life, even after soldiers have retired to normal civilian life. It is only then that the Army would have made a meaningful contribution to the country's general life and character. While chivalry once entailed a precise code of ethics, it has no specific meaning today and provides no guide for our behaviour. It is hardly possible to rally everybody under a particular flag, because honour today is associated more closely with the ethics of an individual soldier, than with any rewards or glory derived from soldierly tasks. Dying for the motherland is no longer a 'war cry' that draws an enthusiastic response from all. The soldier today wants to make sure that his interests are being safeguarded. The world today is unsettled and complex. Economical and social conditions influence both military and governmental leaders where it concerns their armies. In earlier days a soldier was treated with a lot of respect and dignity when he went to his native place. Changes in our value structure has brought about a downgradation of the military from the pedestal of most respected profession to its present state, where soldiers and officers are often treated with disdain, both by the bureaucracy and the politicians. The greater exposure that the soldier has to outside influences is all the more reason that we put our "value structure" under a magnifying glass.

The effectiveness and energy with which a soldier contributes to an entity that is larger than him, depends on either the extent to which he identifies with the objectives of that entity, or the extent to which the paltan (entity) has allowed him to become a part of its structure. All this can be done if you give the soldier *esprit de corps.* Esprit is the sum total of a growing mutual confidence between the leader and the led. It is founded in the faith, that together they are superior to all others and more capable than any other regiment or entity. Comradeship and Regimental Spirit make up *esprit de corps,* which is an essential element of high morale. Without it the most sophisticated and costly military 'hardware' is of little value as the American failure in Vietnam has shown. Once a soldier starts believing in the culture[16] of his regiment, then the reputation of the regiment becomes personal (to be fiercely guarded even at the cost of self-sacrifice) as soon as it is accepted as an honour to belong to that regiment. It is for a commander to create an environment and atmosphere that allows a soldier to consider himself an important and useful member of the community to which he now belongs. All units have a culture, a tradition, and a heritage. One must make an all out effort to preserve it, integrating thoughts and ideas into the common good of the community. All new arrivals should be made to take this as a philosophy of life, with the CO giving the lead. A commander can do this only where the roots are deep and the foundations of his extended family strong.

Thomas J Watson, chairman of IBM says, "Any organisation in order to survive and achieve success, must have a sound set of beliefs on which it premises all its policies and action. The most important single factor in corporate success is faithful adherence to these beliefs. I believe if an organisation is to meet the challenge of a changing world, it must be prepared to change everything about itself except those beliefs that have withstood the tests of time as it moves through corporate life. In other words, the basic philosophy, spirit and drive of an organisation have far more to do with its relative achievements than do technological or economic resources, organisational structure, innovation and timings. All these things weigh heavily in success. But they are transcended strongly by the people in the organisation who believe in its basic precepts and how faithfully they carry them out". A military organisation in order to be successful in withstanding combat stress and other difficulties is truly corporative in nature, except that here "profits and gains" are not measured in financial terms. The success of a unit or a formation is measured in terms of its readiness for and performance in battle. In that, it requires a high level of individual identification with institutional goals as the primary mechanism compelling one's behaviour towards peak performance. It is this very sense of belonging, of sharing common values and of being unique, that defines a truly cohesive military unit. It is these factors which in the end motivate the individual soldier to stand and fight for the *izzat* and *iqbal* of his paltan. These common values are those, which over the years got defined as regimental traditions and customised as drills. Esprit de corps and the brotherhood so essential towards success and regimental glory have to be built into every officer's and soldier's psyche. It comes from having faith and belief in one's mission. It comes from identifying oneself with the rest of the unit, and thus believing that one's own success or failure is directly linked with the performance of the whole unit. In times of crises and when the chips are down, the regimental spirit gets invoked quickly on its own in a well-trained and well-groomed unit. One also has to take note of the fact that sometimes the old advantages of patience, paternalism, and respect for tradition can be hurdles in a world that is rapidly changing. There could be some traditions from the past that do not jell with the present times. This will be particularly so in the case of 'mixed battalions'. In such a situation it is perfectly normal to make changes where required, while retaining the basic fundamentals that have kept the unit or establishment growing over the years.

What motivates and sustains a soldier is a sense of pride in belonging to a Regiment, being part of a good battalion, being led by an obviously competent commander and in having a close association with comrades. In the present day environment, it takes a greater level of mutual understanding and agreement on the social purposes of the regimental structure, for a man to start accepting somebody as his natural superior to guide him and lead him in war. The British had devised a large number of modes and methods in order to ensure the absolute loyalty of their soldiers. Whereas some of them have got outdated with the passage of time and the coming of independence, a large number of motivational and man management measures adopted hitherto fore still remain valid. A brief discussion on various facets is called for, so that we can gain from earlier experiences, and device our own to suit present times.

(a) **Rites and Rituals:** [17] Rites are relatively elaborate, dramatic and planned sets of activities that combine various forms of cultural impressions that often have both practical and expressive consequences. The British created a large number of 'rites and rituals' for different "ethnic groups" that constituted the Indian army. But their intentions and therefore, their methods, were designed to suit the continuation of the 'Raj'. Where tales of valour of ancestors helped, the medium was the bravery of the forefathers and their loyalty to the crown. In the case of more religiously inclined 'natives', religion was made into a rallying point. In fact, their main thrust was to counterbalance "Rajputs" with "Punjabis", "Sikhs" with "Marathas" etc.; this was done with a view to ensure loyalty in the time of crisis and was a lesson learnt from 1857. After independence and with more and more "mixed" battalions coming up with better educated recruits, there are enough grounds for taking a fresh look at some of these motivational pulls of the past. It is important that a unit redefines its culture in tune with the changing times, so that all members of the community can wholeheartedly participate. The focus should be on what one wants to achieve from the regimental "rites", and not a change for the sake of change. That will be counter-productive, because in spite of enlightenment, higher education and a better standard of living, the average Indian soldier reposes a lot of faith in some of the things that he has inherited from his ancestors. 'Rituals' are generally standardised procedures and have set techniques. These are performed in case of specific events and on particular occasions to keep the morale of the troops high. Certain Regiments have elaborate religious and social rituals that do not necessarily motivate and inspire today's soldier to achieve greater glory for self or regiment. Aspects and behaviours that do not conform to today's reality should be done away with, so that the members of a team are not encumbered with unfamiliar and often unwanted events.

The army is an extended family where some shared beliefs have stood the test of time, and there are some that do not fit the modern technology-driven age. In such cases, it might be worthwhile to see that a resolute clinging to custom or tradition does not hinder progress and development. In a better-educated and forward-looking Army, a 'sacred cow' need not be blindly worshipped. Adhering to outdated traditions, which are out of sync with the present times, is not facing reality. What is essential is to see that the 'core' structure of our regimental traditions and our heritage remains intact so that the soldiers can draw inspiration and are motivated to live up to demands that the country and society makes. That is, we have to ensure that the plant of 'regimental spirit' is not damaged but, if possible improved, by re-potting, re-grafting and re-planting.

(b) **Myths**: A myth is a dramatic narrative of usually imagined events used to explain the origins or transformation of something. Also, it is an unquestioned belief in the practical benefits of certain techniques and behaviours that may not be supported by demonstrated facts. Earlier, when troops were normally illiterate villagers, mythical tales of valour or such like helped in boosting their morale and regimental spirit. Today it is not so. Regimental spirit, though a sturdy and strong plant inherited by the unit, cannot be left to look after itself. It must be tended, nursed and groomed. With the educated jawan wanting to know more about certain regimental customs and ceremonies, it is prudent to give him only the kind of exposure that reaffirms his faith in his organisation. Simply giving a new arrival the cap badge, a lanyard and shoulder titles of his regiment will not fill him with its spirit and tradition. It is wrong to think that any soldier privileged to wear the badge and title of a regiment of which he is a member, automatically fills with pride in its traditions and with the resolve to maintain and live up to them. This may well happen, but it often takes time, particularly in 'mixed battalions'. Only historically vetted and proven tales of valour, adventure and those facts that led to the creation of a particular custom should be taken into perspective. Otherwise it could so happen, that someone wanting to know more about a particular 'tale' stumbles onto something that negates an existing theory and belief, and thus makes that custom irrelevant. It is particularly important for older Regiments to carry out fresh and thorough researches into their Paltans' affairs of the past, where an episode happens to be the guiding factor behind a particular custom or even a myth associated with the unit. Unless supported by verifiable historical records, it would be appropriate to tone down prevalent stories of what supposedly happened over two or three hundred years ago, when the ground realities of those times controvert what is being propagated to build up the regimental spirit.

(c) **Regimental Spirit and Symbols:** A symbol is an object, act, event, quality or relationship that serves as a vehicle for conveying meaning and giving a physical shape to the whole perspective. In Field Marshal Slims' words, "the Regimental Colours inspire a more intimate sense of loyalty". The ceremonial trooping of Regimental Colours re-enacts symbolically, the ancient ritual whereby soldiers were shown where the "Colour" would rest by night, to be a rallying point in the event of an attack. It is therefore important that newly inducted officers and men are made aware of the historic and cultural relevance of regimental symbols. That they will have to live up to those symbols will bring in a sense of purpose in all acts and actions of these individuals. A pep talk by a senior helps a new arrival, but he can imbibe the power of that symbol only if he is allowed to feel a sense of belonging. He must be given an opportunity to develop the feeling-a feeling of oneness with the glorious past of the regiment and the events that led to a particular symbol being adopted. Sometimes one finds some senior officers trying to tone down symbols of another regiment because they feel that these have an adverse effect on the 'swagger' of their own regiment or they want to bring in commonality. This should not be allowed to happen because for a Gurkha his 'hat' and 'Khukri' are what gives him an identity that is different. Similar is the case with most of our older regiments.

Their "battle honours" and "colours" are looked up to with dedication and devotion. All of these symbols represent cases of extreme bravery, devotion to duty and courage. There is always a major battle or a military operation where the troops belonging to that regiment displayed their mettle in the face of adversity, thereby keeping the honour of their community, religious beliefs or ethnic virtues intact. Since most of these symbols were earned during the time India was a part of the 'Empire', there are some ill-informed and ill-advised people who want these symbols to disappear. It is also not unusual for some of our more irresponsible politicians to come up with arguments for lowering the colours won by a battalion while fighting, say, Tipu Sultan, or for standing by the British in 1857. To them it makes no sense to keep remembering the sacrifices made by the soldiers for the propagation of the 'Raj'. They do not seem to appreciate that those men had died for their "oath of allegiance" and for the honour of their community or culture. How can we sustain the soldier's will to live up to symbols of valour if we bring in such contradictions and avoidable controversies? (The Americans, after their drubbing at the hands of the Vietnamese, carried out a detailed study to analyse the reasons for their defeat and to find ways and means of improving morale and to motivate their soldiers. A major recommendation was, that the US military adopt the Indian "Regimental system" and educate their soldiers to live up to the hard won colours and battle honours.)

(d) **Develop and display faith in Regimental Saga:** A young officer joining his Regiment after commissioning is impressionable and desperately anxious to measure up to the established norms. He is not critical, as his training and upbringing have geared him to be obedient and ready to accept authority. He is looking forward to becoming part of a larger family than what he has left behind. In this, the seniors can surely help him by educating him about the past of the regiment, that prescribes the standards that the young officer is expected to live up to. The unique accomplishments of our predecessors must become a part of folklore and culture. Almost all units and battalions of the army have their raising days and such like. But with showmanship and a somewhat grandiloquent display of the good things of life being the order of the day, these have generally been reduced to an excuse for social exposure only, where men and junior offices hardly have time for introspection. Instead, elaborate mess functions, a barakhana with the troops and maybe a special sammelan (where a well-crafted speech is delivered in the fond hope of rejuvenating the spirits of troops) are considered to be enough. It is not so. How will a newly inducted soldier or officer take pride in something achieved by his Regiment two hundred years ago, if he is not allowed to absorb the big-ness of the event and the sacrifices it involved? We have to tell him that he has inherited a rich heritage of sacrifice and devotion to duty, and what he has to do to measure up to those standards.

I feel that an over-ostentatious angle given to such great events by some units actually amounts to abusing that spiritual heritage which is expected to motivate the current custodians of the regiment's glory. Formation commanders and Colonel Commandants should forcefully curb this tendency towards expensive raising day celebrations and things like that, because except for the CO being recognised as a hell of a go-getter and jolly good fellow, the unit as such achieves very little in the process. In fact, formation and other higher commanders should refuse to attend such functions so that perforce, the commanders and their teams will have to look inwards and carry out an introspection to see if they are living up to their heritage. Similarly, separate arrangements for officers, in terms of different and better types of liquor and even different food during barakhanas, now prevalent in certain units during these events have to be done away with. The solemnity of the occasion needs to be restored at once, so that the event does not degenerate into a fatigue duty for the other ranks. Informal meetings and friendly celebrations of such events are essential for restoring the faith of the men in their commander's willingness to strive to live up to the glorious heritage that was earned by our ancestors the hard way. The controlled informality of a "barakhana" must therefore be brought back. Simple and straightforward ceremonies will also eliminate the need for the extra duties men have to perform on 'raising day' and other such events.

The things that surround people and provide them with immediate sensory stimuli, as they carry out culturally expressive activities, need to be improved, particularly where it is tinged with historical greatness. It should always be the aim of a Commanding Officer to develop a credo that his men and his officers have to put in that much more effort to perform better than the others in the soldiering facet of their profession, because they have to justify a glorious heritage. This does not mean that a strict yardstick and unachievable goal is set. The 'artefact' that the team builds, should be a monument of professional competence. To develop and create a healthy and wholesome faith, reliance has to be built-in by redefining and redesigning some of our regimental customs and drills. All that it requires is a man's natural faith in his leader and enough elbowroom to be expressive and useful towards the organisational goal of creating an atmosphere that is commensurate with the heritage.

(e) **Improve Physical Environment:** In addition to various celebrations of festivals, we have had healthy tradition of games and sports where men could often excel vis-a-vis officers and thus prove to themselves a streak of superiority. In some big industrial houses, festivals like Holi are celebrated with total and gay abandon on the premise that it allows the lower ranks to let out steam and any latent resentment, in a manner that is not harmful in any way. And the informal setting, involving a physical touch, leads the workers to conclude that the "burra sahibs" are as much mortals as they are, and that they too have similar emotions. Unfortunately, the tendency in officers has generally shifted away from rough and tough games that involve physical contact, partially due to fear of injury, as any permanent "low medical category" could make one unfit for career advancement. Partially, it is also due to the fact that their domestic clime needs more of their time and energy. Today's officer is becoming more of a 'nine-to-five' type of man. His own family and its demands on his time and energies are taking him farther and farther away from the care of his men. When a man has a family he naturally thinks of them, and their well-being becomes his immediate priority. Seemingly, he tends to withdraw from tasks that demand active and total focus on those whom he commands. This kind of a situation can be rectified if officers (particularly a junior leader) are allowed to balance out regimental duties and domestic commitments. What with frequent moves, changes of children's schools, staying away from the family, they certainly need to restore the domestic balance by devoting more time and attention towards their own. But the men they command have an equal right on their leader's time and energies if he wants to be recognised as a competent and caring commander. The question thus is, whether this age-old tradition of having the feet of men inspected after a long route march and a hot cup of tea to them before the officers, is necessary or paternalistic?

"The commander should practice kindness and severity, should appear friendly to the soldiers, speak to them on the march, visit them while they are cooking, ask them if they are well cared for, and alleviate their needs. Small requests should be granted, but severity is maintained about everything regarding duty".

—Fredrick the Great.

If we remember that the Indian jawan, in spite of his improved education, looks towards his commanding officer as the one who is to look after his needs and comforts, the answer will be clear. These are traditional drills that have a lot of meaning behind them. An individual commander will have to find ways and means to meet his domestic and regimental commitments concurrently. ("An officer must constantly interest himself in the welfare of his men and their rations. He should know his men so well that any sign of sickness or nervous strain will be apparent to him. He must look after his men's feet and see that they have properly fitting shoes in good condition; that their socks fit, for loose or tight socks make sore feet. He must anticipate change of weather and see that proper clothing and footgear are asked for and obtained." —General George S Patton, Jr.)

A more subtle approach would be to take an interest in the affairs of a soldier's family. Ask him about the academic achievements of his son/daughter. His face lights up, even in a tense situation, when he starts talking about how his son is busy preparing for the National Defence Academy or entrance to a Medical College. And if a particular soldier has performed some difficult task successfully, write to his family about his good work. The whole unit will soon know about a 'caring' commander and will repay this concern for their well-being with absolute loyalty. A little touch of this kind is, in my opinion, very much more consonant with the requirements of modern leadership. All those officers who hope to lead their men in war, and lead them successfully, have to make an investment in terms of time and effort. These informal norms have to be developed and deeply embedded in our structure so that the officer is eventually in a position to exercise his normal and natural prerogatives on the men he commands. Therefore, every officer needs to make a healthy blend of two conflicting requirements. While it is accepted that an officer has his social, domestic, regimental and professional functions to perform, he must accept all this in addition to his ultimate duty of leading his men in war. A commander looking after soldiers has got to keep thinking all the time. No commander can take his soldiers or his wife for granted. Both require considerable reassurances that he is aware of them, that he is interested in them and that some times he is apt to think of unexpected little bits of consideration or concern for them. It is the duty of the seniors to ensure that their subordinates are not so encumbered that they suffer in this vital personal training need*.

(f) **Institution of "Sainik Sammelan":** The British instituted a very good system where soldiers could bring up points of common or community interest for the consideration of the commanding officer. The Indian Army has continued with this practice and it has done a lot of good as far as raising the morale and performance level is concerned. However, over a period of time, and with modernity catching up, one finds that the 'sainik sammelan' has lost much of its sanctity and importance. So much so, that there are units where the ritual is gone through every month with no point being raised by anybody. This appears to be so because the men have come to believe that raising points marks them as 'trouble makers', as most of the problems pertain to some inadequacy, either on the part of a junior leader or their immediate superior JCO or NCO. During inspections one has seen enough "Sainik Sammelan" books showing "no point" for months on end. Instead of ringing an alarm bell somewhere, this is taken as a certificate that all is well with the command. This is not so. A commanding officer must go into details when this important channel of communication dries up. Maybe junior officers, JCOs and NCOs are trying to restrain soldiers from taking up an issue that concerns them, because a point raised in an open forum may be construed as an aspersion on the immediate commander's concern for the well-being of the men under his command. (As commandant of the Ordnance Depot at Allahabad, when I got 'no point' for three months in a row, I asked all JCOs and NCOs to march out of the 'Sammelan Parade' and then asked the jawans for their problems. The experience was an 'eye opener'. There was so much bottled up anger and resentment against the lack of concern for the troop's welfare that I had to immediately make administrative changes. The problems ranged from timings of water supply to late receipt of personal mail, nothing that could not have been resolved at a lower level.) If simmering discontentment is allowed to grow, it can manifest itself in very serious problems. Some commanders may see sammelans as an opening for the rabble-rousers to embarrass the junior leaders. But this usually happens when the higher commander's disdain for the unit and its officers is not a well-guarded secret. In such situations, all that happens is, it allows the malcontents and the troublemakers to voice their radical ideas, and there are enough of such characters in any army. It will be much better for a higher commander to follow the chain of command.

A leader must understand the basic value structure of his subordinates, so as to obtain maximum effectiveness, because attitudes and values influence our perceptions of the world in such a way as to guide our actions. A major part of the success of a leader lies in his judgement about his followers and their beliefs and values. This is not very difficult to do where units and regiments go far back in time. There, a new entrant joins an establishment where the organisational value structure is easily identifiable and well defined. In the case of 'Service' units like ASC, EME, AOC, AMC etc., it has always been a mix of people drawn from various parts of the country. These services also have a mix of combatants and civilians on their rolls. Their culture can be termed as different from 'fighting arms'. In service units, it is very rare, if at all, that lives of people will depend on the values and actions of others who are their "comrades in arms". It is the combat arms of our army who need to modify their act when contradictions of religion, language and culture manifest themselves, particularly when "mixed battalions" have become the norm. In their case, it has become all the more important to identify the factors that unify the military community. For this to happen, officers and men need to harmonise and share common values and goals, regardless of outside influences generated by the social and political climate in the country. Commanders who want to achieve success in their operational missions must have this aspect as their primary goal because eventually it comes from 'caring', and in understanding the pulls and pressures that bind people into one identity. Education and religion are the two institutional means which the army can employ to help its members to conserve, clarify and extend the practical and specific meaningfulness of historically prized (but sometimes abstract) values. Some commanders may feel that earlier, when the soldier had limited exposure to education, it was easier to mould his thoughts and his mind towards organisational goals. But modern weapons and the technology of today demand higher and better academic levels from the average soldier. This education makes him a discerning member of the community and therefore, much more easy to channelise in a desired direction, provided that direction is the right direction. This is where a commander has to ensure that basic values and faiths are not only ingrained but also, reiterated regularly. Commanders at all levels must keep pace with changing modern society, adapting their leadership style to the demands of the new kind of well-informed and educated soldiers. In fact, there may even be a need for up-gradation of the value structure from time to time, so that no "personality conflict" emerges in an individual's mind. A better educated, more intelligent and imaginative modern soldier must be led with greater understanding than the 'patient' villager of yore.

Montgomery has said in his *Memoirs*: " Finally, I do not believe that today a commander can inspire great armies, or single units, or even individual men, and lead them to achieve great victories, unless he has a proper sense of religious truth. He must be prepared to acknowledge it, and to lead his troops in the light of that truth. He must always keep his finger on the spiritual pulse of his troops. He must be sure that the spiritual purpose which inspires them is right and true, and is clearly expounded to one and all". Wherever a mentally strong person is found, whether an officer, JCO or NCO, his faith assumes great importance to all those around him. Initially it is the comradeship, and finally the regimental spirit which helps men of widely different outlooks on life and environment to live happily together. It is this spirit which often makes selfish, self-centred and rootless men learn to practise unselfishness, and find roots and pride in the traditions of a regiment. Comradeship and regimental spirit are the roots from which good morale grows.

The military represents the host society with which it is converging over time, because of more similar and common technological and other developments and exigencies of our times. This means that the 'higher commanders' need to get an immediate grip of the situation well in time, and guide newly inducted officers towards the basic 'regimental values, customs and traditions'. This they can only do if there is no conflict between their personal ambition and the organisational goal. It will be appropriate to tell a new entrant that the combination of his role in the organisational structure and the goals that have been prescribed, give direction to his personal mission, i.e. to succeed as a leader of soldiers. Informal norms have to be redeveloped where required, and deeply embedded in the army structure so that the officer who exercises his moral prerogative is not degraded or discriminated against by his peers or superiors, or dubbed as being too enthusiastic about his command. However, this change would not take place unless there is a strong support for the new values evident within informal groups in the officer's class. Important to the success of these new values, will be the officer's perception that he is a member of a community. To advance both his 'self' and the organisation as a whole, an officer must perceive a link between supporting the new values and the behaviour they compel. The life of combat soldiers is becoming harder and tougher by the day. Their continued employment on 'counter-insurgency' and other such duties is exposing them to pulls and pressures their ancestors hardly ever experienced. In the US Marine Corps, a new recruit is made to feel, through both words and action, that discipline, hardships and even sufferings are things to be proud of, to look forward to, that virtually nothing is impossible. A commander must be seen to be sharing the privations and problems that the common soldier is facing these days, if he wants to be respected and unquestionably followed by his subordinates. It is worthwhile drilling into our young officer's mind that when the chips are down, confidence and discipline are paramount and complementary; and past actions, good or bad, will be remembered. The emphasis therefore has to be on comradeship rather than on commandership. In short, the officer should begin to identify with the values and codes he and his brother officers, and especially his superiors and subordinates share. Military leaders at all levels have to cope and live with the implications of external conditions affecting the people they are leading. [18]

Chapter 7

Professional Development

"Procedures and processes harness wild horses into working Teams."

—Confucius

One of the most obvious causes of difference in action and reaction to various operational and other functional situations is the degree and quality of training and experience. A combat soldier's confidence rests on three things: his leader, his weapon and his own self. His weapon cannot make him any smaller as a target for the aimed or un-aimed fire of the enemy. More often than not, a leader can do little to guide soldiers once the battle is joined. Only the man by himself, through knowledge of what a trained fighter must do to live and fight, can handle himself as he must if the battle is to be won and he is to survive to relish success achieved in the battle. Only by constant practice can operational effectiveness be ensured. The time and effort a leader invests in a soldier's on job training pays off, not just for the individual soldier but for the unit as a whole as well. All the training and grooming undertaken over a period of time is the only medium available to a soldier to carry out the mission assigned to his unit or sub unit in such a situation. Experience is a slow teacher and the method is costly. It takes the experience of a lifetime to do for a man, what systematic instruction will accomplish during the formative period. As Clausewitz put it: "In war, all is simple-but the simple is still very difficult". The difference between an armed mob and an effective professional army is its training. Military work is teamwork. Teamwork is built best through training.

On induction, an individual is taught the fundamentals of his profession; he learns the basics of military drill, then to drill in a squad and how to handle his personal weapon. Then, he is put through training as part of a sub unit, thereafter in a unit or battalion, brigade and formation. This is how individuals learn to work as a team. Individual training is the first step towards collective training, where different arms and services hone their expertise. This collective training enables a leader to discover his own strengths and of those with whom he works. When trained collectively, each man will have confidence in his own personal skills as a soldier and in that of his comrades, as well as confidence in his weapons and those who are going to support him in battle. Confidence in one's personal weapons, in the supporting armour etc., and in the capability of one's own arm to provide the best facilities to develop professional skills, is essential. It helps in making a soldier believe that he is a better soldier, and has all that is required to win. In a modern day army, such a belief needs to be cultivated. In today's high-pressure environment, no leader can escape the responsibility for training and developing the human resources that he employs and leads. Performance as a unit, and the confidence it generates in an individual soldier, provides the foundations for effective performance at each succeeding level. Training brings in self-confidence. Self-confident leaders are more likely to be assertive and decisive, a trait which makes them gain the faith and confidence of those who will follow them in battle. Every commander should be a positive example to his subordinates while exercising with the troops. This way he inculcates cohesiveness in the sub unit and encourages the soldier to improve his performance. Be it a training event or a routine exercise, wholehearted participation by all ranks is absolutely essential. Officers must have the mental flexibility and imagination to utilise, to the fullest extent, the developments of modern technology. Mao has said that good training and confidence in weapons makes a portrait of courage. Money spent on collective or even individual training is a kind of 'insurance premium' that we pay for safeguarding the vital interests and security of the country. It is for the commanders, at all levels, to ensure that training is given its due place in the scheme of things. At times, formation level training is not carried out for reasons of economy. Or very ambitious targets are set-to be missed, because of VIP visits to the training areas; their briefings and now even 'press parties' have become essential. The accompanying social aspects of such visits shift the focus from the seriousness of the event. There is no doubt that spit and polish have their place in the scheme of things military, but white-washed stone pathways, painted grass and paint on the tree trunks may be carrying things a bit too far. These non-essentials consume a lot of time and energy of the troops and junior leaders. This is a wrong trend. It is easy to fall into a relentless series of repetitive drills and exercises that fail to stimulate thinking and gradually lead to unwanted stress and strain. Higher commanders should insist that the environment remain operational during their visits and inspections, when training is going on. This will help a commander in seeing to it that his soldiers are trained to be in tune with the latest operational requirements. A training event should not be allowed to become a "social event".

Every newly introduced and technologically superior piece of equipment should set hearts aflutter with everyone in the unit wanting to master the latest. Greater capabilities of weapon systems demand much higher levels of skills, that means more and longer training cycles and expenditure, that also means single-minded concentration and minimal distractions for the commander while he is in the training ground with his troops. Instead, what we usually have is a list of who all cannot be spared for training because they are busy elsewhere. In this we tend to forget that the modern war requires trained minds and bodies that can deal with any situation. Armies the world over are moving from the era of 'armed men' to 'manned weapon systems' as a result of changing and improving technology. Training has to be organised in such a manner that an individual is part of a whole where he contributes individually, but in harmony with other segments of his profession. In this millennium, individual intelligence, understanding of a situation and initiative will be far more successful and important factors than weapons or technology.

The performance of an individual on a task depends both on his ability to do a job and his will to do it. Ability refers to the skills in being able to perform a task, and motivation implies his desire to do the job assigned. Today, with the influx of high-tech weapons and equipment in the hands of troops, it has become all the more important that these skills are mastered quickly. A high degree of intelligence and training are required of a man who must move confidently through the complexities introduced by modern technological developments. Training now means long hours of hard work. For the young officers and men, it means not only hard physical work but also intensive study of the training manuals covering the latest techniques required to be mastered for efficient use of their equipment. Commanders at all levels have a much greater responsibility in ensuring that this greater capability in making war is suitably harnessed, so that all the money that the nation has spent in equipping its military, is put to proper use. Obviously, both motivation and ability must be of a high level for performance to be good. Therefore, training in handling equipment, material and resources is an absolute essential insofar as development of professional competence is concerned. In order to be accepted as a leader by his men, an officer must actively participate in all training events and exercises. This will allow him to move in concert with his command when the situation is tense. This will also help him in fitting people into jobs for which they seemingly are best suited. A leader should participate in training and not just be an observer. It does no good to the morale of troops when dog-tired and dirty, they come across a well-turned out, fresh looking battalion or company commander swaggering around, trying to look important and busy.

Bookish knowledge is no good in war. It is only the trained mind and body that has a direct bearing on the outcome of any operation. During training, men learn to have confidence in their officers, who in turn, learn all they can about the personalities and individual aptitudes of their men. More importantly, it is on the training ground that the men see their eventual wartime leader in action and develop faith in his ability to lead. The leader must quickly become aware that his subordinates are watching him to see how he performs under certain circumstances, and how he reacts to unexpected things and situations. He must perform to the best of his ability and indicate that he understands why he is doing certain things. If someone is going to lead, followers want that person to be more capable in some respects than they are. The rule is simple-an officer must study and train and practice until he has more knowledge and expertise than those who are under his command do. That the officer also avoids personal and professional obsolescence in the process is an added advantage.

Professional competence and knowledge is the surest guarantee of self-confidence, self-control and self-discipline. Because of the dangers of war, men must be trained not only for their own immediate tasks, but also to take over other tasks in action so that the effect of casualties is minimised. Equally important for a commander is to train his immediate subordinate to be his deputy in the fullest sense. For a higher commander it is important to identify those of his subordinates who can be groomed for higher responsibility. This will ensure that an effective command continues even if the commander himself becomes non-operative due to any reason. This is in strong contrast to his civilian counterpart, who is sometimes loath to groom his deputy as a successor, in case the deputy should become better at his job than the manager himself and thus threaten his own position. Any leader who can teach his men the things they need to learn and tries to develop the fullest potential of each one will win total loyalty. The time and effort you invest in a soldier's training begins to pay off not just for the individual soldier but for the whole unit as well. This will also help in discovering a potential junior leader, and taking interest in their advancement will bring in automatic loyalty.

Chapter 8

Leadership Training for a Nuclear Battlefield

It is sometimes said that a different kind of soldier will be needed on the nuclear battlefield. This, inter alia, means that the leader will also have to be different from one we expect for a conventional situation. How different has not been specified. It should therefore be instructive to examine briefly how soldiers, leaders and battlefields in a nuclear era differ from conventional soldiering.

In this era of hi-tech equipment, where electronic interference is a technological reality and the chances of an operation turning 'nuclear' are high, junior leaders (NCO and above) may be required to assess immediate situations. They may have to determine a course of action on their own as the aftermath of a nuclear strike can cut off a sub unit. For that matter, an individual soldier may find himself to be the sole survivor, still groggy and disoriented, and required to make a decision with regard to his future course of action. To be able to function independently for any length of time men require a frame of reference that allows them to understand the intentions of their senior commanders, and more importantly, the impact of a 'nuclear strike' on those intentions and plans.

All that it means is that when plans are being formulated, the commander must set only the broad goals and let his subordinate commanders plan their own strategy for achieving those goals. The capacity and opportunity to experiment with unfamiliar situations during training exercises needs to be encouraged so that juniors develop skills for 'rational risk taking' in the absence of effective and immediate guidance in an operational situation.

A nuclear battlefield will create a situation of wide dispersion where communications could fail and exercising of direct leadership will be more difficult. Where lower ranks are concerned, combat soldiers today are likely to be far too widely dispersed against weapons of mass destruction. This wide dispersal will make exercising direct leadership more difficult. During training and exercises, situations should be created where an average soldier is made to face crises needing his initiative and drive. A training event should give him a chance to develop his own instinct for survival and decision-making when there is no one to guide him. It is essential that all ranks be given a detailed knowledge of the weapons which may be used against them and of the nature of the enemy who will be using them. This will help a soldier in overcoming his fears of the unknown. Any effort to look at the entire range of effects merely compounds them. Mainly the uncertainty has to do with the degree of protection available to the troops. Would they get enough warning to make use of the best available shelter? How would they react to the situation? How fast will they be able to regroup for countering the effect of the nuclear weapon? These will be some of the immediate concerns of the commanders.

In numerous exercises carried out by NATO forces, a lot of stress was put on the requirement of troops to operate continuously and at a high level of efficiency without depending on regularly organised lines of communication. An acceptable solution was seen in organising the forces into smaller self-contained units. The commander on a nuclear battlefield will have yet another situation (where troops are concerned) to face in the form of ionising radiation which is inevitably associated with nuclear detonations. The wounds produced by the heat and blasts of the explosion are plainly visible immediately. But those who are affected by radiation may not be immediately manifested. Clearly, if the individual soldier is the determining quantity on the battlefield, then in a nuclear environment command concern for his survival must be greater than it has ever been. In a conventional war medical services are considered to be adequate, because in theory evacuation is only an exercise in logistics. Based on past experience arrangements are made for the anticipated casualties, their transportation and other facilities organised. With nuclear weapons giving another dimension to the scenario, it will be a serious problem for commanders to find sufficient numbers of medicos. There will also be greater emotional stress in situations where the individual may lack close supervision and group identification, where even a remote impact of a nuclear weapon could lead to disorientation. In a nuclear war the Army may not have the luxury of time to make personnel, including doctors, available to handle all kinds of casualty problems realistically. For the moderately and severely wounded, early and effective handling on the field and disposition in the medical channels will give a reasonable chance for survival to most. Care of those who are not seriously affected will be given priority within the operational theatre. This will help in their speedy return to duty and avoid unnecessary depletion of forces. In some cases the casualty will achieve restoration to a degree compatible with a situation where they can be reassigned duty at a future date. Therefore, it might not be a bad idea to include "nuclear first aid" as a training subject at all levels. Besides making help available immediately to a casualty, such knowledge will be good for the morale of the soldiers. It will be better if medical units in the forward areas have attached helicopters as well as tracked and wheeled ambulance vehicles. Returning logistics transport where the situation permits can be used for evacuation of the casualties. Americans carried out nuclear tests in the fifties by creating special cities with human dummies where it was found that underground markets and basements in houses offered the best protection to those who are not caught near ground zero. For those in the vicinity of ground zero, there is no chance of survival.

As survivors emerge from shelters they will need to find uncontaminated food. Their ability to do so will depend on the magnitude of the attack on their physical, physiological and psychological states. As well as the degrees to which needed resources have survived (including weapons, ammunition, food and the means of reconstructing the technological infrastructure) and the possibly changed climate into which they will emerge. Each of these considerations is uncertain. The initial nuclear radiation is an immediate problem. The formation of fallout requires protection of the troops (and the factory workers) for periods of weeks to months. The fallout is usually placed into two categories: Early or local and the delayed (long range) fallout. Early fallout is that which gets deposited on the ground in the first 24 hours after detonation. This time limit is used since the fallout pattern is pretty well established after 24 hours from a single detonation. The following line of action can be adopted:

- **Find a safe and reliable source of water**. This is most essential because. Besides its requirement for drinking purposes, water will be needed for cleaning of contamination from the body parts, decontamination of military equipment and putting off the fires. The human body can be decontaminated by washing with plenty of water. Filtration of water for drinking purposes considerably reduces the radioactivity level.

- **Establish food supply systems.** Immediately after a nuclear strike has taken place the survivors will need to be fed and reassured of the availability of sufficient food. Tinned or packaged rations can be decontaminated by simply cleaning the outer surface. Plenty of these should be made available for distribution. As the civilian population in the area will also be affected, it will be normal to cater for their requirements as well so that regrouping of the fighting forces is not disturbed due to influx of refugees.

- **Establish health and care system.** The medical problems that can arise as a consequence of a nuclear strike have been enumerated above. Sufficient resources must be made available to the medicos to deal with the situation. These resources need not be carried to the battle in the first instance, but should be available at the base and regional depots. Specific transport (including aircraft and helicopters) should be earmarked for conveyance of these stores when called for.
- **Establish search and rescue teams.** The devastation caused by a nuclear strike will cause a large body of troops to be staggered over a very wide area. These men will be totally disoriented and possibly suffering from some after-effects. Formation of suitable and well-equipped search teams will considerably improve their chances of survival and the restoration of their military skills that much faster. Trauma units could be created for dealing with more serious cases.
- **Establish task teams to deal with specific dangers like**:

(a) **Fire, rodents and insects:** There will be a large number of devastating fires spread over a very wide area. Troops in the immediate vicinity of a nuclear strike are not likely to be in a position to do anything to put these fires out. The theatre commander will have to earmark designated teams for this task. For speedy restoration of normalcy, a central pool of manpower consisting of fire-crews, health organisation teams and sanitation squads needs to be created. Here we can make use of our ex-servicemen to beef up the teams so that speedy action can be taken to complete the task with the urgency that the situation demands. Rodents and insects are the most dangerous carriers of disease that lead to avoidable casualties. Disinfecting the affected areas will help in restoring the morale of the local population and that of the troops.

(b) **Pilferage and theft of military stores:** The aftermath of a nuclear strike can create a situation where there is total confusion. Attempts at theft and pilferage will be made by enemy agents or by those who are hostile to the country. A commander will have to organise local defence of the logistics units and areas earmarked for receipt of replacements arriving from the 'base depots'. A commander will be required to detail sentries and night watch at the concerned establishments. This will mean that much more strain on his limited resources. Here again, we could muster our "ex-servicemen" for this kind of duty.

(c) **Contamination:** Nuclear fallout can be removed from most of the equipment by using a water-hose, scrubbing and using washing soap. For delicate equipment, vacuum cleaning is the best approach. The entire range of weapons and equipment which would have come into contact with nuclear particles will need to be cleaned up in this manner, because if left unattended, these could create serious problems for the soldiers handling these, and otherwise unaffected troops could get contaminated. It would not be a bad idea to create special decontamination teams, who should also carry with them a "dosimeter"[$] to measure radiation effects in a particular location and on a piece of equipment. Special protective clothing items should be made available to such teams before they start their task of decontamination. Sector reserves and stocks of relevant equipment can be held at the base depots.

[**Note:** In America, a special agency FEMA- Federal Emergency Management Agency —was created in 1979 specifically to deal with all kinds of situations, including the aftermath of a nuclear attack. We could do the same as this arrangement will relieve operational commanders from the worry of finding men to carry out the above mentioned tasks and from carrying additional material for 'just in case' requirements. All the equipment for the emergencies enumerated above can be held at a central location, to be airlifted to the area where a nuclear weapon has been used.]

(d) **Effects on Morale:** Wide dispersion will ensure that a soldier may not actually see the scenes of mass carnage. But his morale could be affected by the possibility of a thermonuclear war transferring its horrors to his hometown, thereby leading to worries about his near and dear ones. In this satellite era it should be possible to show realistic pictures to the troops as soon as the dust settles. This will help a soldier in arriving at a rational conclusion with regard to his family. Another thing is that the soldier, weary, lonely and isolated may feel that he has reached the limit of his endurance. Even with no one to see, he must have within himself the seeds of leadership, his own personal store of courage and determination. This he can only do if he is allowed to identify his strengths and weaknesses during 'peace time' training, which should be made as realistic as is physically possible.

- **Protection of troops**: The thermal pulse from a low-yield weapon is so short that a man in the open has a very limited chance of survival. However, for a higher yield the pulse is long enough to allow a man to take evasive action like falling flat to the ground, rolling into a ditch or a trench. An all-enveloping cover (like a bunker or a shelter) will almost completely protect against thermal radiation, besides reducing the effects of blast and nuclear radiation. Shelters can be of three types: -

(a) Maximum strength for key installations: Such installations will usually be 'operational headquarters', 'store (including fuel and ammunition) holding units' and medical and allied facilities in the close proximity of operational areas;

(b) Moderate strength for population masses in identified urban centres and factories of strategic importance;

(c) Improvised shelters for small groups and family protection in residential areas in border districts. An effective shelter should be covered with at least three feet of earth. All shelters should have at least two readily available exits. Shelters are also of two further types/classes—blast and fallout. At a distance from ground zero, where blast effects are not so serious, the major problem is of fallout. Different designs are called for to meet different purposes and the expenses will also be different.

The bigger problem however, is that there are far too many uncertainties for a reasonable and workable plan to support a military operation in such a scenario. All that we know is that the environment will be more demanding and uncertain. We also know that it is not possible to provide any textbook answers to leadership and initiative related issues if the environment turns nuclear. All that one can recommend is that individual leaders become more personally resourceful and be willing to take a greater responsibility on themselves.

When the environment threatens to turn nuclear-for a military success with minimum losses-there is a need for continuous and inquisitive search for armaments, better organisation of tactical grouping and reliable methods of administrative support. With nuclear weapons having become a reality, a commander must have the resources required for his task. To meet his logistical and other administrative requirements, special effort and expertise is needed. This is a specialist job. This requirement of military service imposes a scope that is unrivalled by any other enterprise. In fact, in today's environment and with the technological advancements being made in the field of armament and electronics there is a greater need for expertise and a higher level of professionalism in the 'Support Services and Supporting Arms', particularly when things like EMP could render the entire system useless. It will be up to the leaders and technicians to ensure that a high level of morale and functional ability is sustained throughout. The modern war (where a nuclear device could be used) will be fluid, flexible, spread out and consist of many battles fought by small units. This implies that there will be a need for more intimate material support than before, during and after the operations. Tactical logistic problems will be very great requiring maintenance of vehicles and weapons and the rehabilitation of these weapons on an even greater scale than in any previous war. In this, containers can be of very big help as these provide mobility as well as protection to both men and material not in the immediate area of a nuclear fallout.

All the issues highlighted, and those that emerge during training, will have to be addressed at an appropriate level so that an average soldier is confident of surviving a nuclear weapon. Those leaders who are able to solve these problems in peacetime will have greater expectations of success in war, be it conventional or nuclear. A theatre nuclear force R&D programme has to be initiated with the following objective:

"To assess the survivability of various military elements under conventional and nuclear attack, identify deficiencies and develop improvements to develop technology to counter possible future threats to the survivability of these military elements in different theatres of likely military operations."

For a long-range appraisal our lens must widen beyond the immediate future, building the capability to react to a nuclear strike needs a lot of resources in terms of time, effort and money. It also entails preparing the civil population because a nuclear weapon, contrary to a conventional projectile, has very wide ramifications.

In the coming years, with an even chance of a nuclear strike, leadership, particularly at junior level, is going to be far more demanding. Electronic warfare may make communication between units and sub units unpredictable and uncertain. Leaders will have to gather, integrate and interpret enormous amounts of information. These demands are greater than ever today because of the rapid technological changes that are coming about. With night-fighting capabilities becoming more and more predominant, soldiers may be stretched beyond their levels of endurance. Junior leaders will, in all probability, be fighting isolated actions, with little or no guidance or direction from higher commanders once the battle is joined. The ability to function autonomously in a battlefield-where chances of 'command, control, communication and intelligence' failing exist-calls for a shift from our traditional methods of training leaders who will be holding higher assignments in the year 2020 and beyond. It is not possible to predict accurately what the situation will demand at that time, but it is imperative that something more than the traditional and mechanistic methods of training are adopted. Autonomy and initiative, in conjunction with innovation, are called for. A clear, more elaborate and well-defined training and grooming paradigm for leadership at lower levels is called for. Interactive software, where a potential leader is put through a series of battlefield situations, can be employed for this purpose. This will help our junior leaders in grasping the nuances of their job as it is going to be when technology totally overtakes the battlefields of tomorrow.

Right from a section commander to the very top, a military leader, no matter what his level, has to keep learning additional leadership and professional skills as he moves up the ladder. The better each level understands its own particular leadership requirements, the better each level can do its job. This will also harmonise the team and they can work together, giving far better responses and outputs. Teamwork must be both up and down and sideways. For this to happen there must always be more effort towards collective training.

Chapter 9

Is The Leader a Manager?

"Act like a leader, not a manager. Stop managing, start leading. Managers muddle, Leaders inspire. I don't run GE. I lead GE." —Jack Welch

According to John P Kotter, a prominent leadership theorist, today's managers must know how to lead as well as manage. As described by him, there are two factors that demarcate leadership and management:

- Management is more formal and scientific than leadership. It relies on skills like planning, budgeting and controlling. Leadership, on the other hand, involves having a vision of what the organisation can become and how. The manager implements that vision.
- Leadership requires eliciting co-operation and teamwork from a large number of people and keeping the people in the network motivated, using every manner of persuasion.

A military officer is not the direct equivalent of a manager in civil life for several reasons. First, he is not hired for the job but is appointed by the head of state under an oath of allegiance. Second, he can rarely practice any aspect of his profession as an individual. Third, he may be ordered to risk his life in order to accomplish the mission and perhaps to lose it, without the right of lawful refusal. There is no civilian job description for this kind of work. As a commander of troops your responsibility to your soldiers does not end when some whistle blows and a 'shift' is over. Leadership is different from management, but not for the reasons most people think. Leadership is not mystical and mysterious. Nor is it necessarily better than management or a replacement for it. In fact, leadership and management are two distinctive and complementary systems of action. Each has its own function and characteristic activities. Both are necessary for success in an increasingly complex and volatile "functional" environment. Management is about coping with complexity. Leadership, by contrast, is about coping with change. More change always demands more change. These different functions - coping with complexities and coping with change - shape the characteristics and activities of management and leadership. (*"If I were to put in a nutshell the major difference between managers and leaders, it's this: managers run their enterprises as though things will always stay the same and leaders run theirs as though everything will change".*

—Dave Anderson, *in Managers vs. Leaders*)

Successful leadership and good management go hand in hand. Analogies between the Army and the commercial world do not always hold up. Some of the dissimilarities between the two sectors are fundamental and important; others turn out to be not so important. No industrial manager is woken up late in the night when one of his men has met with an accident or is in some other kind of serious trouble. A civilian manager is not expected to have any responsibility towards his workers' families; he is normally not concerned with where they live and how they live. Management and leadership, in a way, are synonymous. The only difference is that attaining military objectives does not require the same amount of judgement at all management levels as accomplishing the goals of a private enterprise. When a decision is made at a certain military level, the main purpose of the organisation is to see that it is carried out with perfection, with precision and on time. Very little time is allowed for the exercise of judgement at the lower echelons, except within a very limited range of alternatives. To suggest otherwise will lead to situations that do not blend with a technology-driven army. There could be any model in operation; but these three factors occur and interact in different proportions. If either dimension is attenuated, combat effectiveness may be adversely affected, so would be functional efficiency in an industrial establishment. One of the great problems today is that amateur and incompetent managers are pressured into using professional management techniques without importing skill or training. The result is fear, defensiveness and ridicule of the technique by managers and a disastrous impact upon the lives, attitudes and work of subordinates.

Leadership suggests an organisation that has unique institutional qualities, resulting from a lifestyle representing a certain kind of regimentation that can be termed as a "calling". Management, on the other hand, implies an occupation or just a "job" where maximizing profits is the main goal. Nevertheless, both are important, since leading of troops in battle and the managing of the organisational systems within which the troops operate, must both be done effectively and efficiently. Management provides the systems, structures and controls so essential to smooth functioning. Things can spin out of control without good management of resources under command.

Managers work with things and numbers. Leaders work with people and their feelings. Leadership is exercised by individuals and not by organisations. Good leadership is a blend of Man Management and Discipline. Where our junior leaders are concerned, it is the amalgamation of the managerial complement in their personalities that sometimes requires filling in, so as to make them ready for dealing with the soldier of today. When they grow in service and attain higher ranks they will have to have their feet firmly on the ground. Leadership is increasingly being viewed as a shared responsibility between the leader and the led. Therefore, consider it a reciprocal process that occurs between two or more people. There is a general agreement that leadership is the art of influencing others to take action towards a goal, and military leadership is the art of influencing soldiers in a unit to accomplish operational missions, where loss of life and limb is a part of the professional hazards. A military leader provides purpose. He also establishes direction, generates motivation and sustains effectiveness till the assigned mission is completed. The military focuses on life and death, whereas business measures profit and success, where the failure of a manager is directly related to his contribution towards that profit. There is a great deal of difference between a great leader and a great manager. Management boils down to the function of co-ordinating the work of others, nothing more, nothing less. "Managers are people who do things right, while leaders are people who do the right things," says Warren Bennis, PhD, author of *On Becoming a Leader*. Dr. Bennis further explains that leaders tend to be more interested in goal direction and in having a vision for the long range. Managers, on the other hand, are more concerned with attending to details, with getting things done today, that need to be done. "Leaders are interested in the 'why' and 'what'," he says, "whereas managers are in the 'how to'." According to him, leadership is not management. **Management is efficiency in climbing the ladder of success; leadership determines whether the ladder is leaning against the right wall.** Efficient management without effective leadership is, as another management guru puts it, " like straightening deck chairs on the Titanic after it has been hit by the iceberg." The key difference it seems is that leaders work hard to develop a strong sense of direction and group accomplishments. While management and leadership are both important, leadership must come first: you must have a direction before you can intelligently decide which managerial systems, structures and controls will best let you achieve your aim.

No management success can compensate for failure in leadership. Leadership is based on a philosophy of life. All this means is that leadership refers to an interpersonal process in a social group, where some individuals assist or direct the group towards the completion of goals and missions. Leadership training and grooming, therefore, becomes different from management training to the extent that it gives lesser importance to the factors that infringe on the main task, that is, training leaders for war and not training managers only to enhance the profitability of an enterprise. There is a debate over whether officers who are being promoted to higher ranks are management-oriented or whether they are "warriors" or "heroes", that is to say, leaders in the traditional sense. Then, there are Arms and Services with their own cultures. Since environment also influences motivation, it is perhaps more difficult for assembly-line workers in our depots and workshops to be motivated than it is in the case of combat arms. In service units there is a mix of combatants and civilians who have their own pulls and pressures, with their unions telling them what to do and what not to do. The commercial world influences their thinking in more ways than one. Naturally, there will be a difference in approach for the two categories. In the case of service units the commander has to blend his leadership skills with those that the management gurus prescribe. For that matter, even a leader of combat soldiers needs most of these skills and traits. For an infantryman or a gunner today has aspirations that were not the requirements of his predecessors. A leader is someone who facilitates change. It, therefore, follows that a leader must be flexible and adaptable enough to cope with change. Meaning thereby, that today a leader is as much a manager of men providing guidance and leadership as a corporate boss.

Command at any level will always be a mix of leadership and management. A formation commander who is in control of men and materials will be more of a manager, but a Captain or a Major will be more of a leader, whom the men will actually follow in war. The leader can only blend managerial skills with his traits so as to motivate his command. It would be appropriate to say that divisional commanders and above are more of managers, as they are sufficiently far removed from the rank and file to influence their actions. It is their management skill that comes into play while motivating and inspiring their command. Just as a painter must integrate perspective and colour to produce his picture, so a higher military commander must balance and merge, push and pull to become a leader. At times, this does not happen. The organisational-technological abilities of the military manager or technician are clearly not the same as the ability to inspire troops in wartime. As the situation exists today, skill and position seem to be mismatched in many cases, and one often finds individuals in positions they are not 'necessarily' qualified to fill.

Military leadership requires management of material resources, and it requires management and leadership of human resources. Put another way, material resources require management and human resources require management as well as leadership. Classical management theories stipulate that for successful utilisation of resources and accomplishment of a mission, one must take recourse to the following:

(a) Establishing the correct relationship between objectives, the tasks involved in meeting them and the resultant grouping of the people required to carry out the tasks for meeting the organisational goal.

(b) Deciding the relationship between authority and consultation so that the organisational head can take decisions based on all the inputs available to him. Consultative leadership requires brains, understanding and the skill to tap the experience and thinking of others, as well as the competency and courage to move in accordance with one's own judgement when the time is right. It also requires considerable humility, human understanding and a sense of the value of individual and group discipline, plus firmness. The only antidote to potential disorder is strong discipline. There is usually an inner relation between discipline and morale.

(c) Deciding the relationship between authority, accountability and responsibility.[19] Leadership must be based on goodwill. Goodwill does not mean posturing, and least of all, pandering to the mob. It means obvious and whole-hearted commitment to helping followers so that they can grow professionally and personally.

(d) Balancing centralisation and delegation of authority. Delegation of authority is one of the most important functions of a leader. He cannot be omnipresent or omnipotent. Delegation of responsibility is a functional necessity. A leader has to delegate authority to the maximum degree possible with regard to the capabilities of his subordinates. By doing so he also instils a sense of responsibility and importance, which comes in handy when the subordinate suddenly has to assume a higher position in a critical situation. Once he has established policy, goals and priorities, the leader accomplishes his objectives by pushing authority right down to the bottom. By doing so, he trains people to use their initiative; by not doing so, he stifles creativity and lowers morale. There are some commanders who are steeped in outmoded tradition and not prone to delegation of duties. They do not realise that the only way a leader can demonstrate that he trusts his subordinates is by delegating authority and responsibility. To shy away from doing so, inhibits your subordinates from sharing responsibility and taking initiative. Strange as it sounds, great leaders gain authority by giving it away.[20]

(e) Importance of communication[21] . Subordinates want to do what the superior wants done - and if they do not, it is because he has done something wrong, because he did not communicate his desires in a manner that could be clearly understood. ("Battles are won through the ability of men to express concrete ideas in clear and unmistakable language. All administration is carried forward along the chain of command by the power of men to make their thoughts articulate and available to others". In *The Officer as a Leader* Brig. Gen. SLA Marshal.)

All the above facets of management are equally applicable to any army unit or establishment. The degree of applicability and relative importance will vary. In that a combat commander, while giving his orders for an assault cannot and will not ask his subordinate's opinion regarding which approach they should take, or whether they take the right flank or the left. He may consult them while planning a particular operation, but ultimately the responsibility will be his. Similarly, a battalion commander would like to retain centralised control of the operation, but he will be delegating authority to his subordinates for various operational tasks. There will be continuous communication between various units and sub units all the time, till the objective is attained. A commander is totally and irrevocably responsible for the well-being and upkeep of his men. His concern for their training and professional grooming goes with the assignment because all commanders have a basic responsibility to ensure that those they are privileged to lead receive realistic training to qualify them for higher responsibility.

One cause for concern is, that an obvious inspiration today is to put into practice, managerial traits in totality for motivating and leading men. (The investigations into American failure in Vietnam have highlighted that one reason why the officer cadre failed to perform, was that since the 2nd World War, the focus of officer training and grooming had taken a totally managerial perspective. Thus taking even junior leaders away from the task of leading from the front.) It is generally not realised, that whereas no body is expected to, or wants to die for IBM, Escorts or TATA, the entire Army exists on this one premise that once the call comes we all are required to give our life for the nation's honour. In any case, what price can really be put on the life of a young man giving himself for his country?

Stephen Covey, a famous management consultant, says that changeless principles such as trust, integrity, fairness, compassion and respect are more important than any fluctuating management skills, practices and techniques. If the focus of the leader is shifted from these basic tenets of leadership, he will be in no position to motivate men for the ultimate sacrifice for the nation. Variations from these tenets only undermine the traditional perspective of community sacrifice and service to one's comrades. Far from being a handicap to command, compassion is the measure of it. Leadership training almost always stresses the fact that the good manager exercises the functions of leadership in order to gain an optimal output level from resources under his control. A managerially oriented commander may come to see his troops as a resource to be used to advance his own career rather than as a moral charge. This charge is placed upon his honour, and rests ultimately in reciprocal trust and self-sacrifice. Some leaders tend to forget that there is no other organisation so dependent on the bonds of trust as the military. One of the difficulties, in fact, in dealing with the question of leadership is the tendency not to distinguish between the aspects of it that relate to making sound military decisions and the aspects that relate to leading men in battle. What is more important is that in a bid to succeed at any cost a commander must not sacrifice his men unnecessarily. There are any number of instances where sensing a major loss of life, commanders have withheld their advances and moved forward only when they were sure of success. Valuing the human lives for which a commander is responsible is one of the fundamental lessons in leadership and must be learnt at the earliest. (*"Unless one values the lives of his soldiers and is tormented by their ordeals, he is unfit to command".* — General Omar N Bradley).

Moris Janewitz, an eminent military sociologist, has pointed out, "There has been a change in the basis of authority and discipline in the military establishment, a shift from authoritarian domination to greater reliance on manipulation, persuasion and group consensus. The organisational revolution which pervades contemporary society, and which implies management by means of persuasion, explanation, and expertise, is also to be found in the military". However by advocating managerial skills and utilising the knowledge of behavioural sciences, it is not implied that a junior or senior leader has to actually placate his subordinates, or that he has to apply any 'sales gimmicks' in order to improve production or performance.

The adoption of business ethics - in their totality - in a military environment has all the potential for disaster, because business ethics are dictated only by 'cost effectiveness', which in turn, is directed solely to the maximisation of profit. An accurate assessment of leadership situations requires a realistic approach to life, people and organisations. No one can acquire the status of a leader by specialising in management techniques alone.

Chapter 10

Industrial Leadership

I once had an opportunity to attend a lecture on Human Resource Management by an American Management Guru. During the course of his talk, he suddenly threw the following question at his audience: "May I ask you, friends, who do you think has been the greatest manager of the 20th century?" The hall remained silent for a long while. No body could think of anyone who could be described as the greatest manager of our times. Seeing that the audience was not responding, the speaker gave a hint. "He was an Indian," he said. That made the situation even worse because how could an Indian be the greatest manager when the world was full of experts who had built industrial empires from scratch.

"You have been wondering who's on my mind," said the speaker: "Well, he was none other the great Mahatma Gandhi." Seeing surprised looks on the faces of the audience, the speaker went on to explain: "Yes, Gandhi was the greatest manager of the century and managers in the United States are always trying to emulate him as their role model. Gandhi was a great manger of human affairs because he never asked anybody to do what he did not do himself. We follow his example and as a matter of principle do not expect our subordinates to do anything that we do not do ourselves. For example I do not expect my subordinates to come to the office on time if I am not punctual myself. No superior can expect his subordinates to do things, particularly if the things he wants done are inconvenient, unless he himself starts doing those things, Gandhi never expected others to follow his dictates without personally setting an example."

The managerial challenge of actually exercising leadership in organisational settings provides "real-world" tests of leadership theory and research. For the practising manager or executive, the triad of traits, behaviour and situations blend together to form a complex challenge. The subtle differences that exist between the military and industry, and therefore, the framework of traits and qualities required in leaders in both of these spectrums have been discussed earlier.

The Army has a fairly large complement of units and establishments where the nature of work, the style of working and methods for motivating subordinates are akin to those that are required in the civil industry. The Commandant of a Base Workshop or that of a Central Ordnance Depot is more of a manager than a leader, because almost sixty to seventy percent of the people working under him are "industrial and non-industrial" civilians. The "Factories Act" and other laws that apply to the civil industry govern these people. The plethora of 'labour unions', with their political and other affiliations keep the leader more concerned with industrial harmony than with productivity. The higher organisational leadership demands production outputs and the workers demand an environment where they can earn their wages without actually putting their hearts and souls in meeting the prescribed targets. A common thread in this kind of leadership and that of a combat commander is that the managerial leader of a depot is required to inspire and influence others just as his combat counterpart. In order to gain an understanding of 'industrial leadership' we need to examine the various roles carried out by a depot commandant because here the officer is more of a manager rather than a leader. With a mix of combatants and civilians under him, leading is a complex activity that requires a wide range of additional skills, as well as the application of skills acquired as a combat commander in a somewhat different manner. To list all the problems a depot commander faces will need several pages. Mainly and mostly, he is expected to produce results with some ill-performing members, while having no or very little control over their performance. He cannot fire an erring civilian worker and yet is held responsible for all that happens in his depot or workshop. Industry also faces the same problem, where 'unions' can hold the management to ransom. The problem is more acute at the floor level because the supervisor hardly has any actual authority over the people working under him. In sum total, a leader here has to engage in a sort of political byplay from three directions: below, sideways and upwards. The people of the great subcontinent of India are varied. It's many different languages and cultures inhibit understanding between various communities and cultures. This is where a leader has to be alert and a good reader of human nature so that he can quickly identify the facets that trigger a desired response from the workers. My experience is that workers in different parts of the country need a different approach because of their attitude and general demeanour. A depot commandant in Punjab is expected to be rustic, even coarse in his behaviour towards workers in order to be accepted as "one of their own". Maharashtrian workers expect to be treated more like equals than subordinates. A fear of God and his wrath tends to motivate workers in UP and Bihar, but they do need long drawn and more frequent "bidi breaks". Assamese and Bengali workers tend to perform better if they are given a time-bound target to achieve. They would want to finish as soon as possible so that they can extend their "rest time". South Indians can easily take offence, even when an innocent and well-meaning observation is made by a superior but has an offensive sound. One thing is common though. An authoritarian or paternalistic style of management will find rejection at all levels. This is so because the workers have been there for years, while a commandant or any high-level functionary will be new to the environment. That is the fundamental difference between dealing with combatants and industrial workers. Here one is expected to be in a consultative and participative mode. Experience tells us that if the higher management is seen to be consulting the workers, particularly when a difficult assignment is to be undertaken, the enthusiasm level tends to be high. One can always word one's requirement in a manner that indicates that the workers' representatives are being consulted. It will pay rich dividends if one can manoeuvre in such a way that the requirement emerges as the workers' idea and not that of the leader.

Motivational Pulls

Ford management once wanted to figure out what combination of factors motivated their employees. They handed each one a list of ten motivational factors and asked them to rate them on a sliding scale starting from the best to the least important motivator. The result was startling. The senior managers' perception of what motivated the employees was at marked variance with the rank and file rating. Appreciation, 'feel-good' and 'hygiene' factors won hands down, while 'good wages' figured somewhere in the middle.

Management's Rating	Rank and File Rating
1. High Wages	1. Full appreciation of the work done
2. Job Security	2. Feeling of belonging
3. Promotions	3. Help in personal problems
4. Good working conditions	4. Job security
5. Interesting work	5. High wages

6. Personal loyalty of the superior	6. Interesting work
7. Tactful discipline	7. Promotions
8. Full appreciation	8. Personal loyalty of superior
9. Help in personal problems	9. Good working conditions
10. Feeling of belonging	10. Tactful discipline

Generally, the following will help in dealing with industrial and non-industrial workers:

A checklist of qualities that make a good leader/manager

1. **Provide clear direction.** An effective leader needs to establish clear goals and standards for those under his command. He must communicate group goals, not just individual goals. More importantly, he must involve his subordinates in setting these goals, and not simply dictate them himself. He must be clear and thorough in delegating responsibility.
2. **Encourage open communication.** The leader must be candid in dealing with people. He must be honest, direct and to the point. Remember that men want straight information from their leader. The leader must therefore establish a climate of openness and trust. In fact, a leader should retain a healthy dissatisfaction with his abilities as a communicator. He must know that eloquence is no substitute for understanding, erudition no guarantee of lucidity, voluble ness no substitute for action.
3. **Be willing to train and to support your subordinates.** This means being helpful to others, working constructively to correct performance problems and going to bat for the subordinates with the superiors. Ideally, middle level and junior leaders should identify with those above and those below by showing a capacity to accept initiations from both, but not to the exclusion of one or the other.

4. **Provide objective recognition.** The leader must recognise men for good performance more often than criticising them for performance problems. Rewards must be related to the excellence of job performance, not to seniority or personal relationships. Often enough, while working under pressure, officers tend to be more and more critical when the response is not quick enough. This only weakens the will of the subordinates. Constructive criticism can be helpful, but positive recognition is what really motivates people.

5. **Establish on-going controls.** This means following up on important issues and actions and giving subordinates feedback on how they are doing. (*"The Commander of an Army neither requires to be a learned explorer of history nor a publicist. He must be well versed in the higher affairs of state. He must know and be able to judge correctly of traditional tendencies, interests at stake, the immediate questions at issue and the characters of leading persons. He need not be a close observer of men, a sharp dissector of human character, but he must know the character, the feelings and the habits, the peculiar faults and inclinations, of those whom he is to command. These are matters only to be gained by the exercise of an accurate judgement in the observation of things and men".* —Karl Von Clausewitz.)

6. **Encourage innovation and new ideas.** The days of unthinking workers are over. If a leader is really willing to listen, he will find that the average worker is loaded with ideas. It will pay dividends if a leader allows his subordinates to try some of these ideas. Individual intelligence, understanding and initiative of the lower ranks can be the most powerful weapons in the hands of a commander. By encouraging innovation and originality on the ground, a commander can experiment with those that improve overall functioning. This will also improve productivity.

7. **Consistently demonstrate a high level of integrity.** Integrity is the most important responsibility of command. Commanders are dependent on the integrity of those

reporting to them in every decision they make. Integrity can be ordered but only encouragement and example can achieve it. An apparently honest and straightforward leader commands immense respect from his subordinates.

The need for human understanding is an exercise of common sense in human relations. There is a time to be stern; and there is a time to be tolerant. This feeling of what is the right approach at a particular point in time is instinctive in some of us and may be lacking in others. But it can be cultivated and developed by all. One just has to observe the behaviour of superiors whom one holds in high esteem, and not that of those who have little regard for prescribed norms.

To Sum Up

"It is useful for a leader to appear merciful, faithful, humane, religious, upright, and to be so, but with a mind so framed that should you require not to be so, you may be able and know how to change to the opposite." —Machiavelli, in *The Prince*

It is fashionable to say that the world is changing fast, but I wonder whether an average Indian really has an idea how fast. We should be very clear about the fact that the forces shaping the world of tomorrow are already in motion. The prescribed code of conduct is somewhat outdated. The institution of military service is in the need of laying down clear and contemporary policies on various aspects of military life. We need to develop a modern approach to soldierly conduct, which emphasises rational self-interest instead of relying upon the dogmatic and clearly obsolete invocations of devoutness and self-sacrifice. An awareness of the ground realities and willingness to adapt will provide a young officer a powerful platform to take off. For today's leader adaptation to changing conditions is the condition of survival. This depends on the simple yet fundamental question of attitude. The Indian soldier was judged by many 2nd World War commanders (including Lord Wavell and Field Marshal

Montgomery) to be the finest all-round man the world has seen. He will continue to be so, to exhibit perseverance and courage in all forms. What is not certain is the high standard of soldierly conduct and that those who lead these soldiers in the given circumstances will sustain courage. An officer who fails will risk ostracism, not so much from his peers as from the 'other ranks', who it seems, have been rather choosy while mentally accepting someone as their natural leader. A famous commander, while defining the Indian soldier, has said that they have been real snobs all along, and have been rather choosy while bestowing their affection on their leaders. A young man who has to lead men in war will definitely want to win their love and loyalty. But the circumstances and the environment demand a lot of adjustments, particularly from junior officers.

Junior leaders are members of the present society. They too have to adopt the prevailing social norms. These norms are not the same as they were when the present day higher commanders were young. In the present atmosphere, the bravery, the courage, the qualities of leadership the young men learn while under training have come under tremendous strain. And yet these youngsters have always elected to live up to and even die for the highest traditions of the military. That shows that basically there is nothing wrong with the quality of our intake and their initial training. It is a sobering thought that the present generation of leaders is more concerned than ever, about culture, values, ethics and good behaviour, in themselves, in their peers and certainly in their superiors. Because of the degenerating ethical climate in almost all spheres of life, they sometimes conclude that there is a lot to be unlearnt if they have to move ahead in their professional life. In the turmoil of our times, every officer will be confronted by situations that test his character. When that happens, must he stand by his principles is what worries a young leader.

An officer could not be a worthy member of this profession if he does not subscribe to certain operating norms of his professional community. He cannot do his duty in a proper manner unless he has courage, selflessness and integrity. These group values are a functional necessity. There is no room for anything other than the common good. And if he wishes to grow in his chosen career then he has to understand that the soldier expects to be well equipped, well trained and well led. No officer can expect to have the respect of his subordinates unless he takes care of them in every which way possible. One cannot be an inspiring leader unless one ensures that the men are provided with the kind and quality of food, clothing and equipment they are entitled to have. They will accept 'hard scales', cold, stale and even unpalatable food when an operation is going on, and when you are undergoing the same hardships alongside. Soldiers accept a lot of hardship and pain if everybody is going through the same together. (Lee Iacocca, a former boss of General Motors, calls this 'equality of sacrifice'.) If one reads the biographies of some of the more illustrious commanders of the past, one finds a common theme that runs all along. That is, "all that a military leader has to do is place the care and protection of his men first, share their hardships; and when the real test comes the leader will find that they have a genuine respect for him and are more than willing to do his bidding".

> *"The general must know how to get his men their rations and every other kind of stores needed for war. He must have imagination to originate plans - practical sense and energy to carry them through. He must be observant, untiring, shrewd, kindly and cruel, simple and crafty, a watchman and a robber, lavish and miserly, generous and stingy, rash and conservative. All these and many other qualities both natural and acquired he must have. He should also, as a matter of course, know tactics."*
>
> —*Socrates.*

Leadership as a concept and as a tool of professional military management must receive more emphasis than any other facet of training and development of a military officer. Morris Janowitz says that as a social organisation, the contemporary military establishment has sometimes tended to display more and more of the characteristics of any large-scale non-military bureaucracy. Taking recourse to a 'safety first' approach, some who have become leaders by default, see only the narrow field of their nose. They do not see what clearly will be required to be done tomorrow. Seeking only to fulfil the expectations of others and to function within pre-defined parameters, this kind of leader finds it not worth his while to champion radically new and different ideas. He is not willing to risk willingly the greater inner resources available to him as a unique individual. For a variety of reasons the military chain of command provides people of dubious talent and doubtful merit opportunities to edge ahead of their more competent peers. Consequently great men are subordinated to efficient men. This condition is one of bureaucratic stagnation. A strong tendency has crept into our system where some officers seem to be developing civil-service type of mentality. They see this approach as a safe route to success and their talisman for further advancement. The ultimate test of any action of theirs is a previous set of actions that have become a method held sacrosanct because, at one time, when things were less complex, it more visibly promoted the general interest. They rarely want to share responsibility. They hardly ever want to decide anything without authorisation. Some committee, group or precedent must be represented in everything they do and upon which they can shift the onus if things go wrong. This bureaucratic mode of human existence destroys heroic vision. This lack of heroic vision makes individuals " all too executives." We do not know how many have taken to anonymity of large scale organisation that the army is as their avenue of escape from the responsibility of decision making and that of leadership in its true manifestation. We need to carry out regular introspection so as to identify the areas that need to be given 'course correction', before circumstances overtake us and we loosen the bonds that made the Indian Army what it has been.

"Without waiting to be marshalled, the soldiers will be constantly willing to perform, without waiting to be asked they will do your will; without restrictions, they will be faithful; without giving orders they can be trusted".

—Sun-Tzu

With constant and regular exposure to the other, and pliable bureaucracy and politicians, an officer is already re-evaluating his ethics and value structure. He is finding that the high standards of personal conduct he is expected to live up to are no more sustainable if he has to advance in his career. In this, seniors have to provide guidelines and direction. It appears that somewhere along the line, some of the military leaders have shifted their focus to issues that are not particularly relevant to the rank and file. This is more so with the higher echelons, where some commanders are taking recourse to intervention by the 'civil courts' and bureaucratic and political connections for personal advancement, rather than spending their energies on the task in hand; that is, providing effective and personalised leadership to the troops. The problem obviously lies in the people and not in the system. A whole army full of eager beavers, all trying to reach the top of the ladder, results in far too many officers concerning themselves with their own advancement rather than caring for their soldiers. In such a situation the leadership cannot be heartening or inspiring. It tends to be perfunctory and dispiriting. An American commander once pointed out that much of what we ask people to do in the army is either dull, dirty, difficult or dangerous and thus a high degree of willingness to subordinate individual concerns to those of the organisation is essential. How many of us are willing to be tested on this statement? To cope with the pulls and pressures of the modern world we need to identify the situations that demand a newer and more dynamic approach. Senior officers going to the courts for redress is already a cause for concern. The sacking of the Naval chief at the behest of his politically correct subordinates cannot be a right lesson for youngsters.

Even with the accepted trend towards the concept of leadership with its emphasis on individual behaviour, leadership ought to be viewed as a one-way process of reaching down through the structure and resulting, hopefully, in upward reaching accomplishment. The skill needed for communicating and motivating is primarily social. Instead of analysis integration and synthesis are needed. Justice dominates, as the principal; economy is secondary.

A term of admiration is to describe so and so as a "tough commander." How often do we hear that so and so is a very tough commander, or he is a very hard taskmaster? Very often the only thing special about him is that he knows what he himself wants. What sets him apart from others is his ability to "see" and put into perspective what ordinary people cannot. He has a vision for the future. This vision is his commitment, a drive and a mission. He sees his objective clearly and then strives to attain it. He lets others know what he wants and what are the fundamentals that influence his policy on any and every aspect that concerns his command. He gives firm guidance and a clear lead. He does what he expects others to do; he is willing to suffer the same inconveniences as his men. A tough commander is "tough minded". He is not a tyrant who rules by fear or intimidation.[22] He is a man who imposes the highest standards of performance on himself and demands them of his subordinates. He is a man of vision who sets lofty goals and pursues them, and he expects others to do the same with single-minded intensity. He is normally an innovator and scorns those who fear change. Mukesh Ambani, now the head of Reliance Empire, is very clear about his philosophy where professional life is concerned. He says, "Think big. Challenge conventional wisdom. Do not fear change or the unknown". Obviously this is one lesson which his father Dhirubhai Ambani taught him, he knew that you cannot go far in life unless you insist on knowing whys and wherefores of things and people. A tough commander is tough because he wants to instill these qualities in those placed under him. A tough minded individual will succeed in any field. Kumaramangalam Birla, the head of Aditya Birla Group, follows the credo that stipulates that vision and ebullience, perseverance, tenacity and a bias for action is what makes one a leader. A tough commander tells his subordinates to have an attitude and a passion to succeed in whatever endeavour the junior has selected to undertake. Tolerant in mind and spirit, he can forgive mistakes but never narrowness of viewpoint and selfishness. He will ensure that those put under him strive to achieve standards he has set for himself and his organisation. He will ensure that those who are placed under him realise that the toughness of his approach is for the ultimate good of the organisation and the individuals who form that organisation. The men always respect such a commander because they are convinced that he has 'their' good in his mind, and living up to his expectations will only help an individual in his personal and professional growth.

Good leadership cannot be impersonal or depersonalised, detached or aloof. A leader has to immerse himself totally in the task of minding his men. Serving the motherland and the glory of dying for the country are no longer motivational pulls for a large number of those who are joining the military. We are going through a phase of 'value transition', and due to greater awareness and higher education, maybe a phase of 'value dissension'. Assuming that the traditional military values are still applicable, it is for the seniors to guide new entrants in the right direction. This puts a tremendous responsibility on the shoulders of the senior officers in our units and establishments.

There is a strong military tradition that vests considerable authority, responsibility and accountability with the commanding officer. At the unit level, one man's personality and efficiency are decisive in creating the spirit and character of his command. If a major war continues to be avoided - and it should be avoided - the profession of soldiering could be weakened from within, unless we set ourselves to think wide and deep. There is a case for greater concern by the higher commanders where avoidable loss of life and limb is concerned. The Indian soldier is still undemanding, loyal, hardworking and dependable. This has been amply proved during the Kargil operation where the Indian soldier retrieved heights ranging from 12,000 to 18,000 feet. There were all kinds of limitations. The inadequacy of equipment, lack of training for fighting in high altitude areas, limited resources etc., were no hindrance for these brave men. That the territory was wrested back with a considerable loss of life is a well-known fact. It is also well established that if the men had proper clothing and equipment these losses could have been reduced. How long we can expect our soldiers and junior officers to keep accepting risk to their lives because of situations other than the merit of the case is anybody's guess.

Quite a few of our regulations and restrictions are outdated. But we continue to lean heavily on them, knowing that the times have changed and the soldier is no longer an illiterate villager who can be lured into situations for which there is no rationale. He will follow orders; for that is what he has been trained to do. But he will resent this lack of concern. Leadership has its inspirational side; emphasis on this aspect alone tends to divert us from recognition of the actual skills required to elicit the desired performance from the complex organisation that is characteristic of a modern army. When under-equipped and underfed soldiers are expected to do battle in extremely inhospitable terrain and areas, mere words and exhortations are not going to be enough. The commercial world has similar considerations where it involves humans and human relations. There is a common factor running through the activities of the industry and the military. This common factor is that people are closely associated together under direction to accomplish certain stipulated and well-defined purposes.

"For a leader to secure commitment from his subordinates", writes Abraham Zaleznile, "he has to demonstrate extraordinary competence or other qualities that subordinates admire. If the leader fails to demonstrate these personal qualities in his role, by tradition the leadership compact begins to disintegrate."[23] The Army cannot tolerate young entrants who fail to grasp the subtle nuances of the profession of military leadership. The army needs honourable men. It needs them on the battlefield, where an officer's word is unquestioned. It needs them in peacetime to manage a large and costly organisation. The army needs honourable men to set an example both within the army and to the nation. This has become all the more important because the army is getting more and more into domestic turmoil, which is not going to fade away in the foreseeable future. Human Rights specialists and other do-gooders waste no time in espousing the cause of this militant group or that violent set-up, so that they can draw political mileage from these misguided youth who have elected to take up arms against the State. In the process, far too many frivolous complaints are made against our soldiers and officers. This mudslinging, besides lowering the morale of the troops, causes tremendous damage to the military fabric. Since in a democratic environment it is hardly possible to quieten these lobbies, the army will do well to insist upon having a neutral observation group at the national level. The army should task this group to take up any "alleged" violation of human rights. Speedy investigation and action, if a valid complaint is found, will do a lot of good to the community as well as to the military.

The Peters and Waterman study, *In Search of Excellence* lists eight attributes of a successful leader. These are:

- Active participation. Do it yourself until it works.
- Responsiveness to the commander. Do whatever the commander needs done.
- Power down, cultivate initiative and the freedom to try.
- Achievement through the effort of others. The rank and file are the source of quality; reward it.
- Performance, excellence. Be the best that you can be.

- Adherence to the mission. Define the individual's mission in relation to the organisation's mission.
- Simple form, lean staff. Communicate to solve the problem without letting layers of staff or organisational charts confuse the communication.
- Centralised planning decentralised execution. Solve problems at the lowest possible level; planning originates at the top, but permeates all levels.

The stability of the environment is today under stress from different quarters. With long-drawn CI operations and other commitments, the army has become more of a machine, perpetually in motion with no end in sight. This causes extreme personal turbulence because the 'peace tenures' for the combat soldiers are constantly declining. There does not seem to be an immediate way out that could ameliorate the situation. That makes it all the more challenging for higher commanders. It is for them to tell the average soldier that what he is being made to suffer is important and in the national interest. The cutting edge of the military (or for that matter of any organisation) in the coming years would be how swiftly and effectively it will be able to recognise the potential of its biggest resource–manpower-and recognise that this resource has feelings, ambitions and hopes, unlike machines. The biggest mistake most managers (or leaders) make is forgetting that excellence comes from people who care, not from a good reporting system or other system of control.[24]

It is worthy of repetition that no one can develop a leader. No one can predict what and how he will do in given circumstances. We can, however, offer him full opportunity for development and ascertain that he has what he needs to do the job well if he wishes to do so. Military leaders need to develop the stance, capability and skills that will enable them to firstly, manage and then provide leadership to their men positively and effectively in the years to come. The way these future officers are educated, developed, trained and employed within the military structure eventually gives ethos and values to this profession.

"I have three precious things, which I hold fast, and prize. The first is gentleness, the second is frugality, and the third is humility, which keeps me from putting myself before others. Be gentle and you can be bold; be frugal and you can be liberal; avoid putting yourself before others and you can become a leader". —Lao-Tzu

Notes:

1. "Leaders must be seen upfront, up-to-date, up to their job, and up early in the morning". Lord Seiff, Director Marks & Spencer, England.
2. Jack Welch, CEO, General Electric
3. In his book *"The Managerial Mystique"*.
4. BH Liddell Hart *"Thoughts on War"*, 1944.
5. "By a careful cultural design, we control not the final behaviour, but the inclination to behave-the motives, the desires, the wishes." B. F. Skinner.
6. "Carefully study the well being of your men, and do not overtax them." Sun-Tzu *"The Art of War"*.
7. "Leadership Styles in Army at Junior Level During Peace and War" Indian Management" December 99.
8. "Soldiers must be treated in the first instance with humanity, but kept under control by means of iron discipline. This is a certain road to victory. If in training soldiers, commands are habitually enforced, the army will be well disciplined. If the general shows confidence in his men but always insists on his orders being obeyed, the gain will be mutual". —Sun-Tzu *The Art of War*
9. "Given time and adequate guidance, junior officers are forged into mature professional soldiers in the only way possible: by experience." Major General Aubrey Newman in *Follow Me*
10. "One of the common ways that seniors induce self-defeating stress in their juniors is to over-supervise them. Another is to summon them repeatedly to report in person about inconsequential administrative details." Maj. Gen. Aubrey Newman *Follow Me*
11. "Originality is the most vital elements of all military virtues". —BH Liddell Hart.

12. "In a regiment 'culture' is a learned way of living, transmitted from one person to another down through the years. It largely remains unchanged in its basic structure and has a pattern that is easily identifiable.

13. Our calling is most ancient and like most other old things it has amassed through the ages certain customs and traditions which decorate and ennoble it, which render beautiful the otherwise prosaic occupation of professional men-at-arms."

—George S Patton, Jr. $

14. "Integrity without knowledge is weak and useless, and knowledge without integrity is dangerous and dreadful" —Samuel Johnson.

$ Dose Rate Meter or Dosimeter is a device that indicates the total radiation dose. Safe limits have been prescribed. This helps a combat soldier to avoid radiation effects while he is engaged in clearing an area where a nuclear device has been used.

15. Accountability is defined as the hard cold understanding that a man does his job or gets out of it. Responsibility is the obligation of a person to carry out the assignments and functions given to him by a person of higher authority.

16. Vice Admiral James Bond Stockdale in *Military Ethics*

17. "Without knowing the force of words, it is impossible to know men." —Confucius, circa 500 BC.

18. *The Management Mystique*.

19. "The principles of leadership in the military are the same as they are in industry or anywhere else: (a) Learn your job, (b) Work hard at your job, (c) Train your people, (d) Inspect frequently to see that the job is being done properly".

—Admiral Hyman G Richover.

Appendix

The Will of Marshal de Belle-Isle

(Translated by Major (US Army) Larry J Brown)

Marshal de Belle gained prominence during the War of Austrian Succession, 1740-1748, and was active in reforming the French Army. The following is a letter he wrote to his son on the duties of a military commander after his son was selected to command a regiment.

The regiment that God has just given you is one of the best in the army. Its lieutenant colonel is a soldier respected for his long and excellent service; all of its captains are older than you, and there is not a one of them who, if his personal services had been considered, would not have merited more than you being named colonel. However, it is you who will be their commander; let this first thought never leave your memory.

I will not tell you: seek to merit the esteem of the corps that you are going to command, for this maxim is too trivial. But I will tell you: seek to merit its love. Every colonel who has won this precious sentiment obtains things with ease, even the most difficult, while he who has not acquired it only obtains things with great difficulty, even the most simple. Make yourself loved therefore, my son, and the difficult role of colonel will become for you an easy game. You would deceive yourself greatly if you were to imagine that, in order to obtain the love of your regiment, you should let discipline slide or give in easily to the desires of each of your officers; this method would be neither certain nor glorious. You would also deceive yourself if you were to imagine that a sole virtue, however brilliant or fortunate it might be, can win this sentiment, as it is not only the eyes of a woman which captivate you. It is the totality, the sum of her traits, it is the same with the combination of virtues and knowledge, of which I will speak to you in this document, which will gain for you the love of your regiment.

Have, therefore, for your lieutenant colonel the greatest respect; give no order without consulting him. I have often given you this advice, this command; I will do so again each time I find the opportunity. If following the example of certain young commanders you lack respect or consideration for your lieutenant colonel, you would cause me to have the most unfavourable opinion of you, and you would soon become the victim of your imprudence. Your regiment, divided between you and him, would be easy prey for cliques and factions, and from then on, you could no longer hope to do it any good.

Have marked respect for the older captains, consult them frequently, show them friendship and confidence. Be the support, the friend and the father of the young officers; love the old sergeants and soldiers; speak to them often and always with goodwill, even seek their advice from time to time. A commander of troops will always profit from this popularity; it has often been useful to me.

Study and know profoundly all the officers of your regiment. Deprived of this knowledge, you would be deceived each day. You would confuse modesty with lack of talent, confidence which comes from the belief in one's strengths with vain conceit, desire for order with malicious criticism, love of good and justice with snooping and accusation, envy or excessive ambition, moderation with apathy or indifference, and severity with inflexibility. You would take advice prompted by flattery or self-interest as if it were based on truth; you would believe yourself to be rewarding virtue, but these rewards would fall upon intrigue; thinking yourself to be favouring real talents, you would only be extolling apparent or artificial ones.

When, after having studied the officers of your regiment for a long time, you know them all, you will choose between the eldest two special friends in whom you will have recognised virtue, knowledge, love of truth and order. You will confide in them the important task of speaking freely to you of your faults. And of showing them to you clearly. Listen to these officers with attention and tractability; however, keep from giving them exclusive or blind confidence and from showing too clearly to the rest of the command the preference you give to these two officers. This knowledge could become the source of animosities.

I will tell you never to employ with your soldiers heartless words, dishonourable oaths, and never use profanity or degrading language in their presence. The colonel who uses these expressions with his soldiers degrades himself, and if he is speaking to his officers, he commits an extremely evident blunder. Never forget that the officers of your regiment are men, and that you must, consequently, employ a tone and language when giving them orders that are suitable to those persons in whom honour is the motivating factor. Understand clearly, my son, that this method is the only good one, that only it can make your orders respected, make them acceptable, accelerate their execution, and inspire in the soldiers that confidence in their officers which is the key to good discipline and success.

Never use punishments that the law forbids or the national spirit condemns. When you must punish, let all the pain that you feel to be forced to take such extreme measures be visible on your face. Never miss the opportunity to render small services to officers of your command; in waiting for momentous occasions to oblige them, you risk never being of any service to them. As it is the small kindnesses which retain affection, look often and hard for chances to request medals for your officers, sergeants, and soldiers. The government may refuse your requests, but they will know your sincerity by the warmth that you put in your requests, and your regiment will love you the more for it. Never lead on any of your subordinates with hopes that you have no possibility of fulfilling. When the persons who hold them see them dashed, they will accuse you of having neglected their interests.

I have accustomed you, over a long period of time, to rising at four in the morning. Keep this fortunate habit. You will never have a greater need of time, because you will never have so many studies to do and duties to execute. Having attained the grade of colonel very young, you will be, or so it appears, a general officer very soon. There is no better time, therefore, to devote yourself to the study of the great tactics of war. You must learn them now. But no matter whether you arrive at a grade higher than that which you now hold, believe me, my son, the duties of a colonel require the most varied and extended knowledge. Can you hope to judge the talents of your corporals if you do not know, as well as the most intelligent among them, the sequence that one must follow to train a recruit? Nor can you judge the knowledge and skill of your sergeants if you do not know the full extent of the duties with which they are charged. What I am telling you of the sergeant is equally applicable to the lieutenant, to the captain, to the major, to the lieutenant colonel. Yes, my son, it is only by making yourself capable of finding all the different positions subordinate to your own that you can fill in a worthy fashion that which has been confided to you, and to force the others to carry out all their duties.

I will not recommend to you the study of military regulations, because you undertook that at an early age, but never deviate from what they prescribe. I will be the first to punish you or to request your punishment if I ever learn that you have permitted yourself to stray from them. The law is, in the eyes of every good citizen, of every good soldier, the most sacred subject. It is said, I know well, and in my youth I said it as well as did others: "The letter of the law kills and the spirit brings to life." But as I have always seen that, under the pretext of this theory the greatest transgressions have been permitted, I order you expressly to hold to the letter of the law. Also respect the customs which have been in effect for some time. If you find among them, however, one, which is abused, then it must be abolished, but proceed in so doing with care and wisdom. Prepare by your conduct and by your words the changes that you want to put into effect, and make their advantages felt. Never undertake the destruction of several abuses at once. Begin with the most significant, the most essential. If one attacks at once all portions of a structure one wishes to reconstruct, one always unsettles it and sometimes even topples (it). Do not demolish without having prepared that which must be put in the place of what you wish to topple. Remember that one always does more harm than good when one proposes without consideration even the most advantageous changes, and when one uses violence to have them accepted. Consult the experienced officers concerning the reforms you want to undertake; they will bring, in the wake of their opinion, that of the entire command.

I will not speak to you at all here of the study of war. I have already demonstrated to you the advantages and the necessity of this in a memoir that preceded this one, and I indicated to you the plan you must follow in order to learn this science. I will limit myself to reminding you that history is the source on which you must constantly draw. Do not read history to learn history, but to learn war, morals and politics. History has been, ever since my childhood, the object of my study, and I owe to it all that I know. Do not neglect mathematics; I am displeased with myself for not having studied this subject enough. I learned it early, I liked it, I made progress, and I owe much to the little I know of mathematics.

You are brave; you have proven it, but keep yourself from being so to excess. How many tears have cost me the bravery of someone, who was so very dear to me? Let your bravery be less cruel to me. Bravery, which is the most important quality of a soldier, must, in a colonel, be tempered by caution. However, I would much rather have to mourn your death and your glory than your honour. Remember that those who advise you most often to spare yourself would be the first to blame you if you follow their advice.

Love your country, love your king, you must, my son, both because that is a duty imposed on all citizens, and because the medals which have been awarded me make it a law for you. These feelings are etched in your heart deeply enough that I can dispense with chiselling over them once more. Love glory; let the desire to obtain it always be ardent. This passion for glory has sustained me in the difficult career that I have led. It made me forget that I was born of delicate health and frail body.

I will not speak to you of honesty, but I recommend to you that you watch over that of your troops. Some colonels are accused of selling positions in their regiments. I do not believe that this can be. They give them away, but their men sell them.

Have a regiment that is superior and better trained than the others, this vanity is permissible to a colonel, but do not seek to make it a thing of beauty or to overload it with ornaments. See that your companies are always full of men ready for war. Let no false pity allow you to permit your captains to receive the pay of the soldiers so that they have none. He who permits himself this embezzlement deceives the king and lacks honesty. You also lack it if you do not use the most exact fairness in the distribution of awards and if you do not insure that your subordinates are not making illicit profits at the expense of your soldiers. This attention, my son, is one of the principles that a colonel must have.

Never let yourself be driven by impatience or anger. One always regrets having followed the first dictates of his emotions. "If you wish to do something foolish, follow the counsel of your anger" correctly observed one of our poets. It is in heeding anger that a commander sometimes compromises his honour, sometimes his life, and even more often that of the men who serve under him.

Obey the laws and the men that the prince has chosen to carry them out. Insubordination is, in the first place, the greatest of military vices. It spreads like wildfire and it becomes stronger as it is diffused. Can any colonel who does not obey his superiors expect or hope to be obeyed by his subordinates?

Consider yourself the judge, the headmaster, the magistrate and the father of your regiment. As judge and magistrate, you will watch over the maintenance of moral standards. Concern yourself particularly with this objective, always forgotten or too neglected by military commanders. Where there are high morals, laws are observed, and what is worth even more, they are respected. Look to purifying morals but do not think that they can be established through orders. They must be taught by example and inspiration. The power of the example is here, like almost everywhere, stronger than that of will. Vigilance would have us discover, in vain, vices in others with which we ourselves could be reproached. If your morals are pure, those of your regiment will be also. Your temperament will be fortified, you will save much time, you will be sheltered from numerous ridiculous things, and you will never be the victim of circumstances, and public esteem will compensate you for the deprivations you will have imposed upon yourself.

Avoid gambling, and especially games of chance. Banish them from your regiment. They are the ruin of many soldiers. Keep yourself from developing a taste for wine, for it stupefies. Your mess should be well prepared, but never delicate. Admit into it the officers of your corps, giving preference to general officers, colonels and other commanders. In your mess, let the places be marked according to the degree of esteem that your table guests merit.

Reduce your trains to the bare essential. You must give the example of simplicity, of modesty, because you are the colonel and because you are my son. This moderation will be less difficult for you since I paid the greatest care to prepare you to avoid the excessive softness that transforms the majority of young soldiers into delicate women. I never allowed gold or silver to be placed on your horses, your mules or the uniforms of your men. I hope that you will continue to practice this necessary simplicity.

The opulence that is so fitting of a man charged to represent a prince is dangerous to a soldier in general and fatal to a colonel. His command makes it a duty, an honour, to imitate him. I have never seen, without extreme indignation, the young commanders of your regiments dragging the luxury and the softness of court after them in camp and in garrison. Seeking to make themselves distinguished by the richness and the brilliance of their trains, a horde of valets, the beauty of their horses, the delicacy of their mess. All these officers do is to rival one another in the art of sensual pleasures. Is this the ambition that should motivate military commanders? I have said enough. Bitterness would soon cause me to be carried way. In any case, my advice to you is less necessary on this point than on many others.

You have never seen a man suffer without strongly desiring to make his ills disappear or to lighten them. Keep my son this sensitivity. It may well cause you difficulties from time to time, but it will more often bring pure pleasure. It is as much for your glory as for your honor that I recommend that you show yourself to be humane and generous. Humanity and liberality win and conserve for us the hearts of the men with whom we live and whom we command. Whatever it costs you to aid suffering humanity, I will provide it with joy. I prefer that they speak of your charity than of your skill at organising celebrations. Let them be surprised at the number of people you make happy as opposed to the number of high and mighty ones that you try to entertain. The memory of a celebration that you have given leaves neither in the mind nor in the heart any agreeable trace; that of an unhappy person whom one has consoled leaves most delightful thoughts. I am not at all opposed to your distributing, on some important occasion, a general reward to the soldiers of your regiment. However, I would prefer that you spend the same amount of money on those who have been wounded, who have accomplished some feat of bravery, or who in fulfilling their duties, have suffered a loss which to them is significant. Never allow a single week to go by without visiting once or twice the sick of your regiment. Speak to them kindly, listen to their complaints and respond to them, hear the details of their injuries. This obligingness will contribute as much as medicine to hastening their healing. Visit often the prisoners of your regiment. A guilty man must be punished, but not locked up in an unhealthy place. I do not tell you to spare in war the blood and pain of your soldiers. He, who exposes them to unnecessary perils, in order to advance his own reputation, is unworthy to be called a man. You should know also that the glory that one obtains at such a price is neither desirable nor lasting.

French colonels have long been renowned throughout all of Europe for their politeness. I am certain that you will not injure this reputation. Far from remaining below the level of your models, you will surpass them. The majority of colonels are only polite with women, their superiors and their equals. You will be so with those below you. You will never speak to, or of the officers of your regiment with the imperial tone which certain commanders affect. I repeat, remember that many of your subordinates have earned more than you the right to command a regiment. Many have a more ancient and illustrious family than yours. The only thing they have lacked in not having been placed over you is a little wealth or good luck. Therefore, be accessible, affable, polite, considerate, but even more so, towards your subordinates than towards your equals. Politeness with one's equals is often no more than skilful politics, while that which one exercises with his subordinates is proof of goodness of heart. The praise that I have received for never having caused the weight of .my authority to be felt should encourage you to follow my example.

If you ever make any mistakes, be quick to admit and especially to correct them. While this manner of conducting one's self is totally natural and is not deserving of praise, it will however draw praise for you, will win you hearts and will allow you to pardon mistakes in others. I have often experienced this myself. Pay special attention to the young officers of your regiment. Watch over their conduct yourself, as well as their training and their habits. Be, as I have told you, their father, their support, and if necessary, their teacher. Your regiment will be no better than the training of neither your officers nor its constant zeal for the service. Believe me when I say that you will only obtain these results by paying strict attention to the young officers, and by making them acquire proper habits of conduct quickly. Act in such a manner that the old officers feel for the young the tenderness of a father for his children, or at least that a teacher has for his pupil. Insure that the young officers have the proper regards, respect, and condescension for the old officers, like well-raised children have for their father. Create and maintain unity in your regiment. Hasten to snuff out discord before it takes root, to rid it of animosities, or at least to head off its destructive effects. This is one of the prime and most essential obligations imposed on colonels.

Only have recourse to other eyes or to other hands when it is impossible for you to see everything, to do everything. Delve into all the details. One only knows things well when one knows their smallest parts. It is not for colonels to see only the big picture. However, do not look to take charge of those details which regulations have given to your subordinates. Content yourself to observe that each one of them is fulfilling his duty properly.

Finally, here is my last precept: Always remember, my son, that it was not for yourself that you were made a colonel, but for the good of the service and the regiment which has been confided to you. Let the glory of the nation thus be your primary preoccupation.

"Know your Men —-

Know your Business —-

Know yourself ——"

Bibliography

1. *Crisis in Command* by Richard A Gabriel and Paul L Savage
2. *Top Class Management* by Richard Graham and Edwin Singer
3. *Management in the Armed Forces* by John Downey
4. *Military Leadership* by James H Buck and Lawrence J Korb
5. *Before the Battle* by Lt. Gen. Edward M Flanagan, JR.
6. *Small Unit Leadership* by Col. Danridge M Malorie
7. *Leadership* by James MacGregor Burns
8. *The Art of Administration* by Ordway Tead
9. Leadership *When Heat is On* by Cox and Hoover
10. *Morale - A Study of Men And Courage* by John Baynes
11. *The 7 Habits of Highly Effective People* by Stephen R. Covey
12. *Military Leadership*-Edited by Robert L. Taylor and William E. Roseenbach
13. *Leadership on the Future Battlefield*- Edited by James G Hunt and John D Blair
14. *Motivation and Leadership at Work* -Richard M Steers, Lyman W Porter, Gregory A Bigley

15. *The Effects of Nuclear Weapons* - Edited by S. Gladstone and PJ Dolan (US Department of Defence and Energy publication). This is a standard reference for the effects of nuclear weapons. Chapter v is on damage from air blast, Chap vii is on thermal radiation and Chap ix is on nuclear fallout.

16. "Effects of Nuclear War", *Journal of the Federation of American Scientists,* 34 (No2 1981)

17. *Nuclear War-Survival Skills* by Cresson H. Kearny

18. *Jack Welch and the GE Way* by Robert Slater

19. *Akira Sueno Entrepreneur & Gentleman* —A Case History of a Japanese Company: Translated by Neal Donner

20. *Beyond The Last Blue Mountàin* (A Life of JRD Tata) By RM Lala

21. *The Practice of Management* by Peter Drucker

22. *Human Relations in Management* by SG Huneryager and IL Heckmann

23. *Vedanta and Management* by Nalin V Dave

24. *Are You Communicating?* by Donald Walton

Index